The Tai Chi Flipbook

written by
Craig Balcom

Editor
Photography and Concept by
Kirk E. Bales

Flipbook Publications
Thousand Oaks, California

DISCLAIMER

Please note that the authors and publishers of this instructional book are **NOT RESPONSIBLE** in any manner whatsoever for any injury which may occur by reading and or following the instructions herein.
Before beginning any exercise program be it gentle or intense in nature, and including the program described in this book, it is essential that you consult your physician to determine your level of physical fitness.

ISBN 0-9652261-2-3

Printed in the USA

First printing
June 1996

CONTENTS

Print in bold at the top of the page is instructional and refers directly to the photograph.

Print in stylized font at the bottom of the page is supplemental and does not directly relate to the individual photographs. It can be read sequentially and is divided into three chapters:

PREFACE

The authors' hope is that this book can do what no other Tai Chi book is capable of doing: actually enable a reader to learn the movements of the Tai Chi form. The film-like illusion created by a flipbook allows a reader to see the necessary transitions and progressions which any other type of book would omit.

And it's not just a picture book. The text provides all the necessary philosophy, background and history relevant to the study of Tai Chi Chuan. It also Includes a new interpretation of the Dao De Jing, an important book of ancient Chinese wisdom which goes hand in glove with the study of Tai Chi.

Tai Chi successfully integrates the mental and spiritual benefits of yoga with the physical benefits of a martial art. Of what use is mental calm and spiritual bliss if the longevity and health of the body are not equally developed? The practice of Tai Chi reduces stress, creates good posture and balance, promotes health and healing and provides a new way of looking at and experiencing your world. It is truly meditation in action.

Those who practice Tai Chi are said to have the wisdom of a sage, the vitality of a lumberjack and the suppleness of a baby. Can tens of millions of practitioners be wrong?

ACKNOWLEDGMENTS

Thanks to Sydney Sims for swift and painless editing, to Susan Ackermann for art and support, to Dan Kallen for advice on Chinese matters, to my teacher Paulie Zink for teaching me true Kung Fu and to my students without whom I would never have learned so much.

Craig Balcom 1995.

Thanks to Craig Balcom for being patient and understanding and for sharing your art with me. To my two wonderful stepchildren Tessa and Austin who bring richness to my life every day. And most of all to my wife Dr. Stacy Claire Sutherland for her loving support.

Kirk E. Bales 1995

ABOUT THE AUTHORS

Craig Balcom has been studying Tai Chi for fifteen years. He has a black belt in Hapkido and for over a decade has been a student of Master Zink in the arts of Tai Shing Pek Kwar Kung Fu and Daoist Yoga. In 1993 he won first place at the Long Beach Internationals for his form work. He has been teaching martial arts and yoga in Thousand Oaks California for almost ten years, where he now lives with his wife Susie and step daughter Tessa.

Kirk E. Bales is employed as a motion picture studio grip, he is currently working on the television series "Wings" and "Ellen". Kirk has been practicing martial arts and yoga for five years and considers himself a serious student of Tai Chi.

CREDITS

Kirk E. Bales:	Editor/Publisher: Original concept, photography, page layout and cover design.
Craig Balcom:	Writer/Publisher: Instruction, Philosophy and Dao De Jing.
Sidney Sims:	Text editing and proofreading
Susan Ackerman:	Illustrations
Dan Kallen:	Consultant on Chinese affairs
John Dechene:	Macintosh consultant

CHECKLIST

You will want to try to:

1. Breathe deeply and evenly through your nose, and with your diaphragm.
2. Keep your knees bent.
3. Be very relaxed.
4. Keep your elbows down and your shoulders rounded.
5. Keep your back straight and tuck your pelvis under slightly, like a dog with its tail between its legs.
6. Keep your head balanced as if supported by a string stretching from the top of your head to the ceiling.
7. Keep your wrists and hands relaxed and sensitive.
8. Keep your weight on one foot at a time.
9. Move slowly as if through water.
10. Move the body, breath and mind as one harmonious unit.

How to use this book

1
Hold the bookbinding
in your left hand.

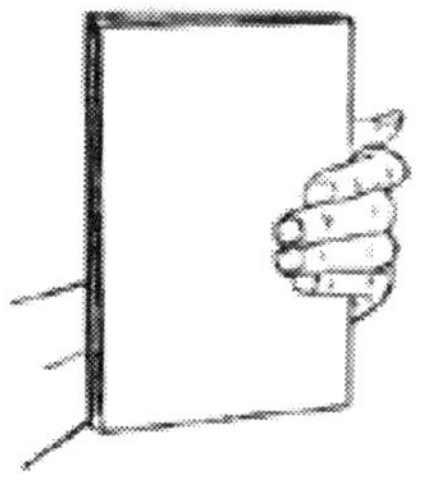

2
Turn the book over.

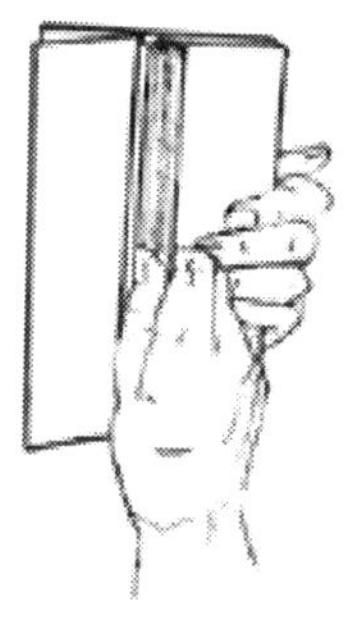

3
Flip the pages right to
left with the right
hand.

Turn the book over and repeat steps 1, 2 and 3.

The Tai Chi Flipbook

and Dao De Jing

1 OPENING OF TAI CHI

Relax, feel your feet on the floor. Have a calm and quiet mind.

Tai Chi means supreme ultimate and refers to the grand universal process, or 'HOW' the universe works.

415 END OF TAI CHI

Straighten the legs.

2 OPENING OF TAI CHI

Inhale deeply, expanding your abdomen to do so. Always breathe through your nose. Expand your belly as you inhale, contract your belly as you exhale.

This process can be understood as the cyclical, harmonious inter-action between positive Yang and negative Yin poles.

414 END OF TAI CHI

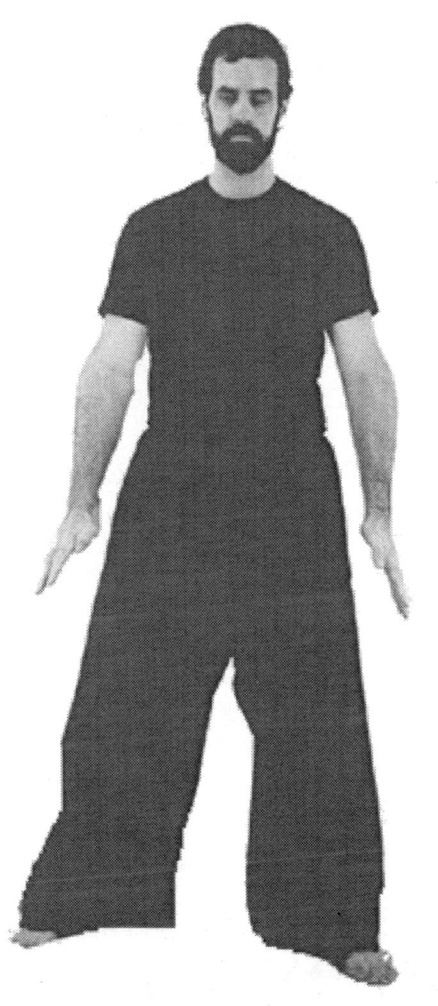

Be still for a moment as Tai Chi returns to a state of Wu Chi.

The sage possesses nothing. The more he gives, the more he receives. With all the ruthlessness of heaven he does no harm. Without doing he does the most.

3 OPENING OF TAI CHI

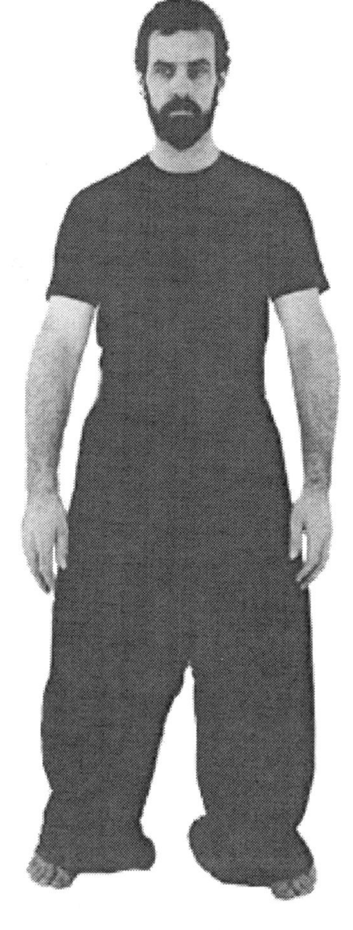

Sink the body, rest heavily on the feet as though you were sitting on them. Continue inhaling slowly. You will never hold your breath.

Symbolically in the form to inhale represents Yin activity, to exhale represents Yang activity, and so the act of breathing represents Tai Chi.

413 END OF TAI CHI

Keep the knees bent; relax and exhale.

81

True words are
not refined;
refined words
are not true.
Those at one
with the Dao
know the
truth and
have no need
of argument.

4 OPENING OF TAI CHI

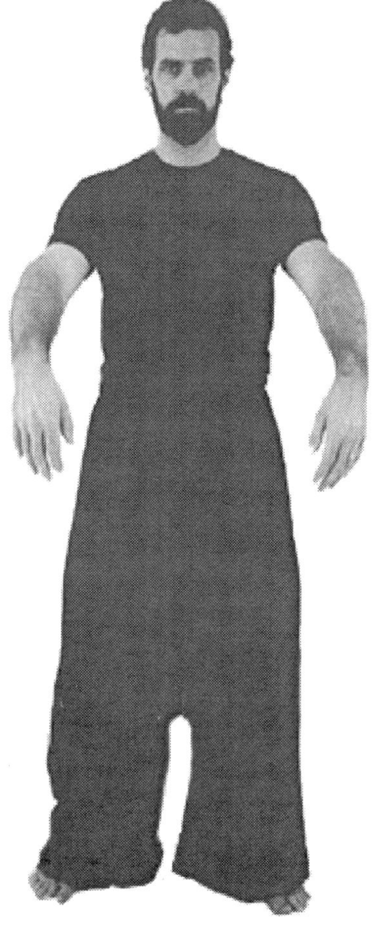

Begin to raise the arms.

Activity is Yang. Passivity is Yin. Tai Chi is the blending of active and passive.

412 END OF TAI CHI

Place the weight evenly on both feet and let the hands drop.

Happy people would consider their everyday life a source of pleasure. Nothing could ever tempt them away from it.

5 OPENING OF TAI CHI

Exhale and raise the arms to shoulder height. Keep the wrists relaxed and the elbows bent. Slightly straighten the legs.

Wu Chi is the state before Tai Chi, the nothing that comes before something.

411 CLOSE UP

Cross the hands but leave a space between your arms and body.

80

If a small community is governed well, not even disaster can make the people leave.

6 OPENING OF TAI CHI

Inhale and pull the elbows back, but not too far. The elbows will always stay in front of the chest.

Wu Chi is represented in the form by putting the weight on both feet equally.

410 CLOSE UP

Withdraw the right foot and set it down shoulder width from the left foot.

The sage keeps an open mind. Those at one with the Dao see the whole picture, not just what benefits themselves. Heaven is indifferent and therefore is always on the side of truth.

7 OPENING OF TAI CHI

Exhale and push the hands down to the waist. Sink the weight back down, bending the knees.

Shifting the weight from foot to foot represents Tai Chi. The weighted leg is Yang, the empty leg is Yin.

409 CLOSE UP

Lower the hands.

79

When two sides dispute can both be right? The sage will separate his ego from the matter; he would rather be effective than right.

8 WARD OFF LEFT

Shift the weight before you begin your turn.

A forward shift is usually Yang movement, a backward shift is usually Yin.

408 CLOSE UP

Separate the hands and shift the weight to the left foot.

The sage will yield before life's trials and in so doing rise above them. Truth is a paradox.

9 WARD OFF LEFT

Round the arms and the back, depress the chest; your wrists are straight and fingers relaxed.

The breathing, the shifting of the weight, and the intent of the movement all determine whether the movement is Yin or Yang.

407 RAINBOW

Turn in the left foot as you continue to arc the hands across the face.

78

Nothing in the world is as soft and yielding as water and yet it carves canyons from solid stone. The soft overcomes the hard; the weak conquers the strong.

10 WARD OFF LEFT

The right foot picks up and moves right. The right toes point to where the eyes are looking.

The breath, shift, and mind are congruent: all three Yin, or all Yang.

406 RAINBOW

Shift to the right foot and begin to turn the body to the right.

People will take from those with too little only to increase their own abundance. Only those at one with the Dao can act without thought of reward and can succeed with humility.

11 WARD OFF LEFT

The hands relate to each other as if holding a ball.

The form flows from Yin to Yang and back again. The cycles are continuous, even and smooth.

405 DOUBLE PUSH

Follow through.

77

The Dao is like drawing a bow. The high is brought low and the low is raised up. It adjusts too much and too little, creating perfect balance.

12 WARD OFF LEFT

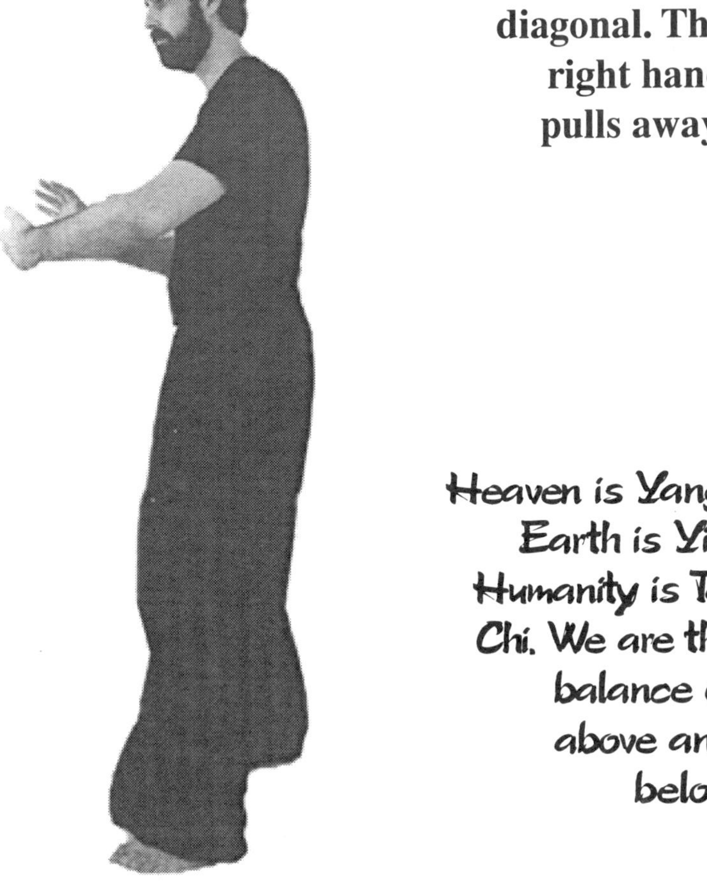

The left foot steps to the forward diagonal. The right hand pulls away.

Heaven is Yang. Earth is Yin. Humanity is Tai Chi. We are the balance of above and below

404 DOUBLE PUSH

Shift forward.

Those who rely
on strength will
not prevail and
the tree which
is strong
courts the
woodcutter.
Therefore
mistrust
strength and
honor softness.

13 WARD OFF LEFT

This is the actual posture of ward off. It is the first posture and shows the basic rounded nature of the arm and shoulder girdle which is maintained throughout the form.

The shoulder girdle and arms represent heaven. The waist is humanity. The lower body, legs and feet are earth.

403 DOUBLE PUSH

Lower the hands and drop the elbows.

76

Babies are supple; corpses are stiff. Saplings bend with the wind; dead branches break off. To be supple and yielding embraces life. To be stiff and resistive courts death.

14 WARD OFF RIGHT

The right arm will start to wave up in a small circle. The right foot will begin to step forward.

Keep the weighted leg firmly rooted in the earth and imagine a thousand-pound weight hanging from your tailbone.

402 DOUBLE PUSH

Circle the hands up and in front of the face.

People do not mind dying if their life is too hard. It is best to leave people alone so that they may find their own joy.

15 WARD OFF RIGHT

Try to harmonize the arm and leg movement.

Keep the head and spine stretching upward and imagine a string running from the top of your head up to the heavens supporting you like a puppet.

401 WITHDRAW

Slide the right arm over the left palm.

75
The people starve when those who rule feast. The people rebel when their governors command too much.

16 WARD OFF RIGHT

The hands will act as if catching and holding a ball.

The waist is supple, relaxed and responsive. It coordinates the upper and lower body.

400 WITHDRAW

Open the right hand and shift the weight to the right foot.

Those who try to control others through fear are like babes with sharp tools: they will surely cut themselves. Only the Dao can elegantly guide our lives.

17 WARD OFF RIGHT

Step down heel to toe when moving forward, toe to heel when stepping backward.

Power begins in the legs. It is controlled by the waist and is emitted through the arms.

399 WITHDRAW

Slide the left hand under the right elbow. Turn the right fist up.

74

People who live in fear will never live harmoniously. Nothing is utterly controllable.

18 WARD OFF RIGHT

This is ward off right. The left hand presses down.

The root and weight shift empower the waist by torquing it.

398 PARRY AND PUNCH

Follow through; punch with the weight of the body behind the fist.

The Dao overcomes without striving, obtains answers without asking. Its net is large, its meshes far apart but there is nothing it does not catch.

19 ROLL BACK

The left palm, right elbow and right palm form a triangle.

Like a drawn bow the waist stores, then releases the energy without effort.

397 PARRY AND PUNCH

Shift forward and bring the left hand to the right forearm.

73

Those whose courage is demonstrated as defiance rush to their death. Those who demonstrate their courage by yielding live on.

20 ROLL BACK

Be as soft as you can. Roll back demonstrates the basic quality of yielding in the form.

The arms are like arrows shot from the bow of the waist.

396 PARRY AND PUNCH

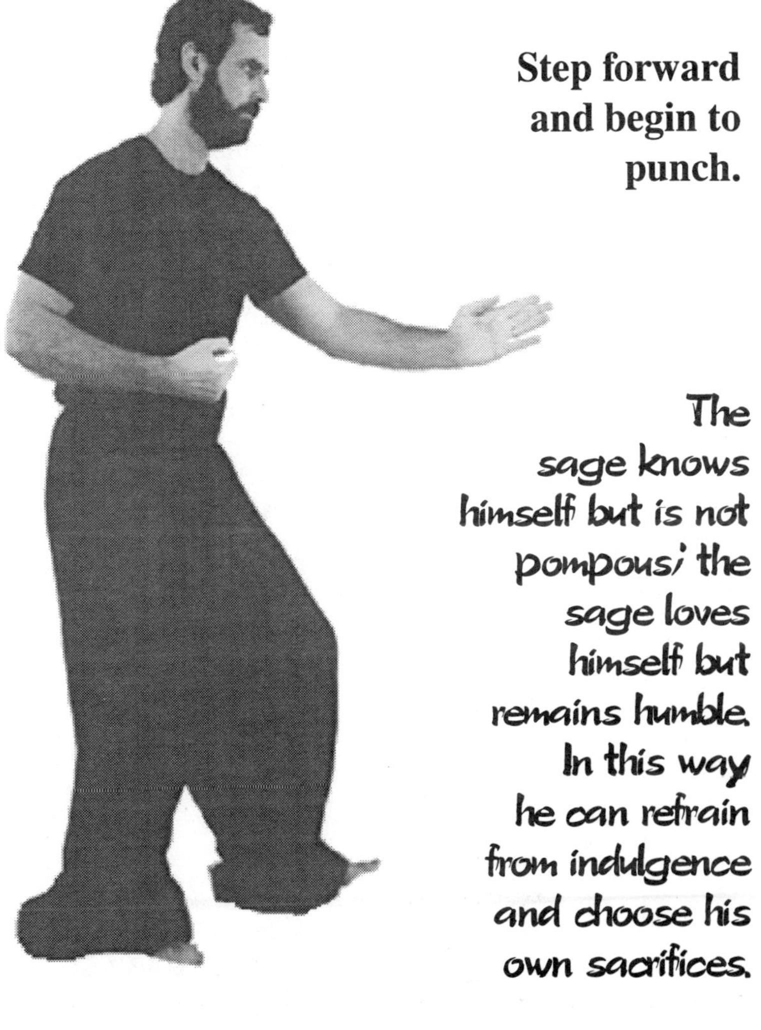

Step forward and begin to punch.

The sage knows himself but is not pompous; the sage loves himself but remains humble. In this way he can refrain from indulgence and choose his own sacrifices.

21 PRESS

The tips of the left fingers press up to and support the right arm.

The arms generate no force of their own.

395 PARRY AND PUNCH

Shift forward and extend the left hand.

72

When people do not fear dying they forget that living involves sacrifice. When people overindulge in life's pleasures they lose interest in life's necessities.

22 PRESS

Do not extend the hands beyond the toes.

Keep the back straight. Align with the pull of gravity.

394 PARRY AND PUNCH

Set the foot down heel first and with the toes turned out.

The sage knows the pain of self-delusion. It is this pain that keeps the sage from believing that he owns the truth.

23 DOUBLE PUSH

Relax the hands completely. Begin to draw back.

Heaven flows straight through you to the center of the earth.

393 PARRY AND PUNCH

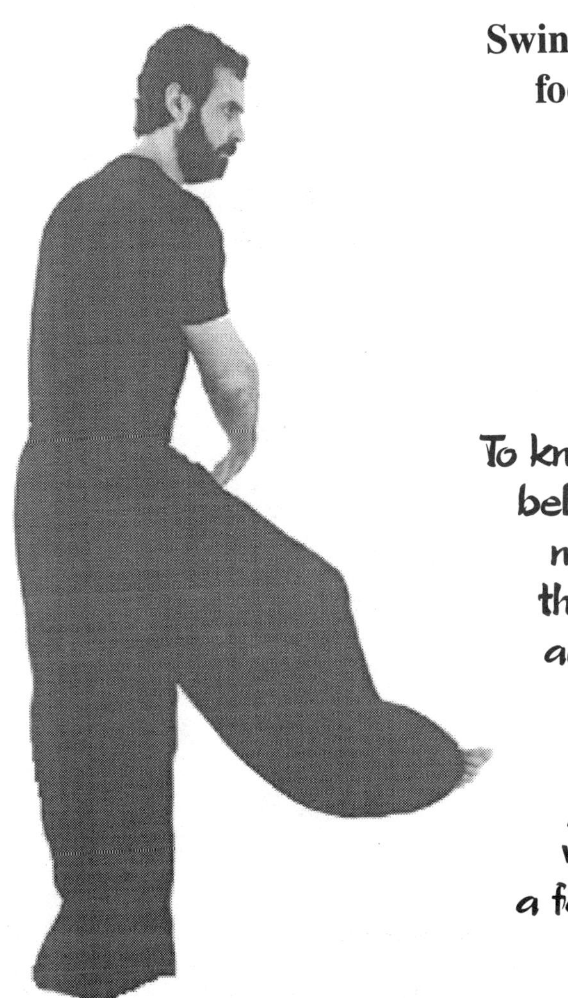

Swing the right
foot forward
and out.

71

To know and to believe we do not know is the greatest achievement. To not know yet believe we know is a fatal illness.

24 DOUBLE PUSH

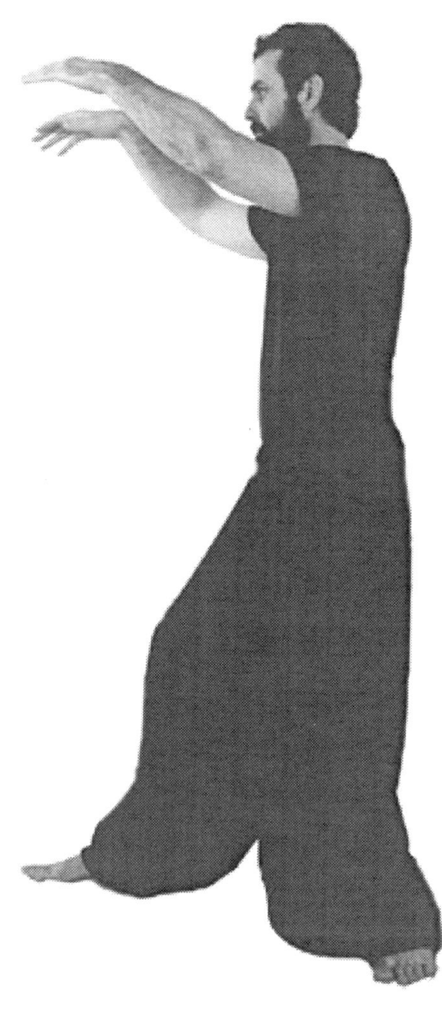

Rise up only a little. Keep the hands and wrists relaxed.

Earth energy can be expressed as rooting, solidity, passivity and calm.

392 DEFLECT DOWN

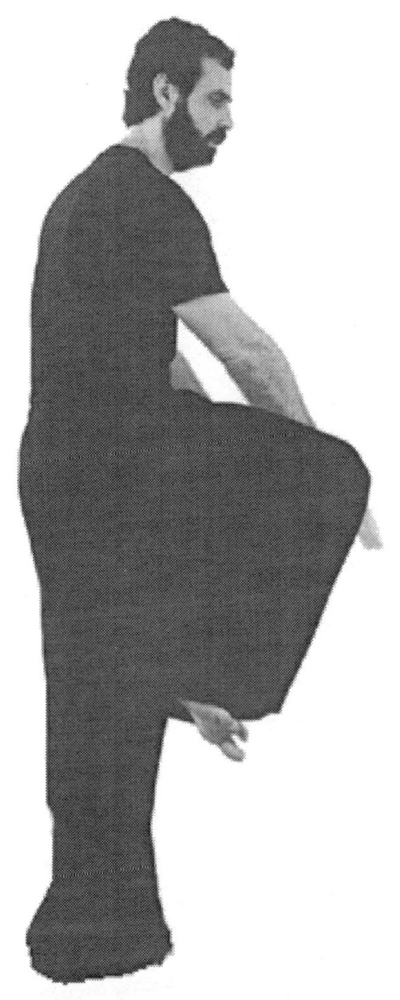

Recoil the kick while deflecting away from your lower body.

There is all the universe in these words and because few understand them they are like rare gems. It can then be said that the sage wears rags on his body, but keeps diamonds in his heart.

25 DOUBLE PUSH

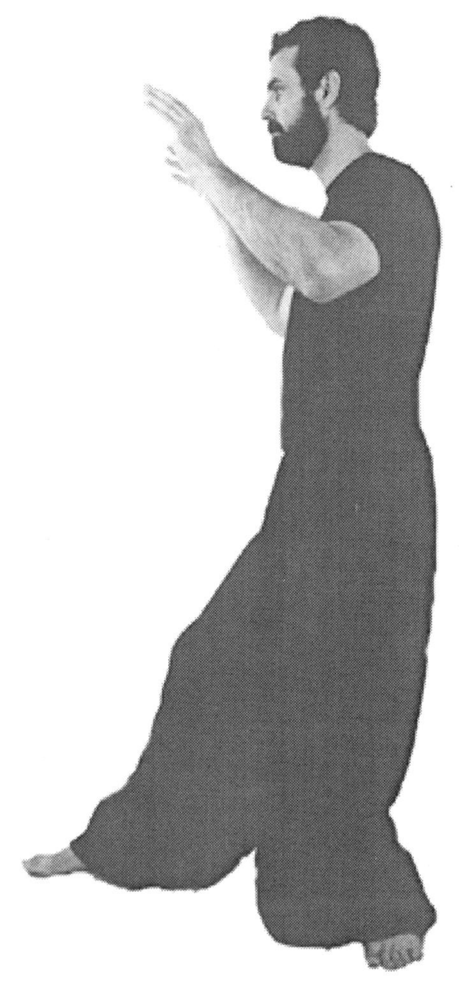

Sink down a little extra, as if you are turning a wheel.

Heaven energy can be expressed as permanence, consciousness, activity and alertness.

391 TURN AND KICK

Bring the hands in and down.

70

These words are easy to grasp and easy to try. But no one truly knows and practices them.

26 DOUBLE PUSH

Stay low and push only with the body.

Human energy can be expressed as mediation, balance, flexibility, coordination and being alive.

390 TURN AND KICK

Kick with the heel.

There is no greater tragedy than the enjoyment of conflict. It kills our compassion. And so when battle is engaged the one who yields will win.

27 DOUBLE PUSH

Do not extend the push beyond your knee.

Qi means breath or breath energy. It is the force that animates all life.

389 TURN AND KICK

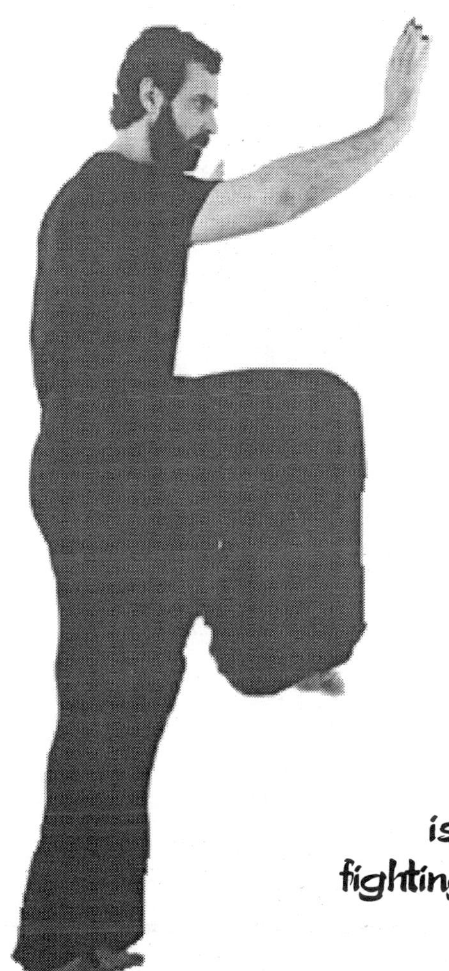

Keep the shoulders relaxed and rounded.

69

In war it is better to defend than to attack. It is wiser to retreat than to advance. This is called the art of fighting without fighting.

28 RAINBOW

Pivot the right toes inward with your arms.

Qi can also mean any kind of energy or force: human, natural or mechanical.

388 TURN AND KICK

Separate the arms and begin to lift the right knee.

The way
of the Dao
is the
way of not
contending.
To yield and
harmonize
has
always
been
the best
way.

29 RAINBOW

Keep your elbows relaxed and make a nice arc with your hands.

Human Qi has three aspects. They are called Jing, Qi, and Shen.

387 TURN AND KICK

Shift the weight to the left foot.

68

A skilled warrior is not warlike. A good fighter is not violent. The greatest conqueror is not contentious. The best ruler is the humblest servant.

30 RAINBOW

The right foot turns in so far as to be pigeon-toed.

Jing refers to tangible procreative energy, the semen in males and menstrual blood and ova in females.

386 TURN AND KICK

Keep turning and cross the arms.

Prize these three things: compassion, frugality and humility. Only from them spring courage, generosity and achievement. Compassion conquers all, and protects the compassionate.

31 RAINBOW

Place your weight on your left foot.

Qi flows through us. It is replenished by the breath.

385 TURN AND KICK

Spin on the right foot and set the left foot down with the toes turned in.

67

It is the greatness of the Dao which makes it appear inferior. Do not confuse subtlety and simplicity with inadequacy.

32 SINGLE WHIP

Bring all the fingers of the right hand together in a hen's beak.

Shen is consciousness and can exist outside the body.

384 TURN AND KICK

Swing the foot forward and inward.

By going last the sage goes first and none can reproach him.

33 SINGLE WHIP

Begin to shift to the right leg. Keep the foot pigeon-toed.

The body is like a light bulb. Qi is like the electricity. Shen is like the light and heat emitted. Jing is like the energy that would make new light bulbs.

383 TURN AND KICK

Bring the left foot back and out to the side but do not set it down.

66

The seas receive the waters of the rivers and streams because they are lower than they. So the sage who wishes to be above places himself below.

34 SINGLE WHIP

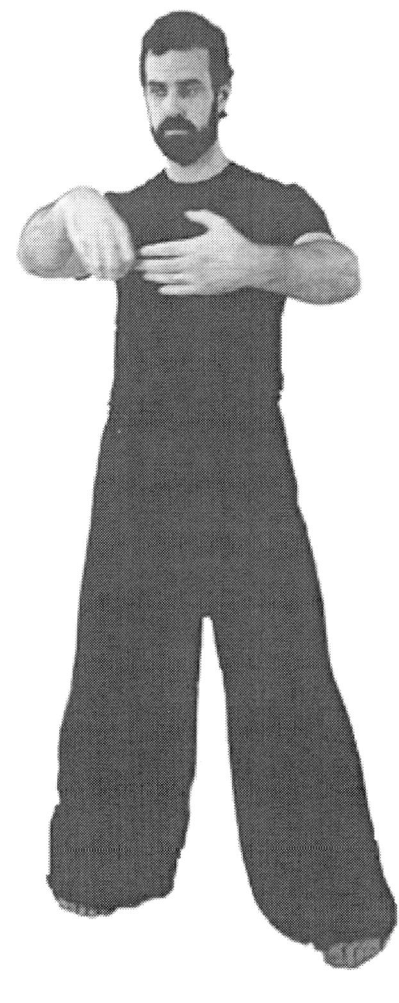

Swing your elbow smoothly back.

The Tai Chi form is like the switch that turns on the light. The mind is like the hand that flicks the switch.

382 KICK LEFT FOOT

Recoil the foot.

The best teachers teach by example and follow their own teachings.

35 SINGLE WHIP

Shift the weight completely to your right and extend the right hand.

Jing relates to earth. Qi relates to humanity. Shen relates to heaven.

381 KICK LEFT FOOT

65
The best
teachers teach
how to know
nothing. Those
who know it all
cannot learn.

36 SINGLE WHIP

The right arm is not quite straight.

Jing has the solidity of earth. Qi has the transitory nature of humanity. Shen has the permanence of heaven.

380 KICK LEFT FOOT

The
sage
desires what
others do not. He
prizes what others
despise. In this
way he helps
the natural
course of events.

37 SINGLE WHIP

Keep your supporting leg bent.

The Tai Chi form balances and regulates the flow of Qi.

379 KICK LEFT FOOT

Kick out with the heel.

The harder you grasp the more it will slip away. The sage will be flexible and harmonize with events. He is as careful at the end as at the beginning.

38 SINGLE WHIP

To maintain balance keep the back straight.

Correct breathing while doing the form strengthens the Qi.

378 KICK LEFT FOOT

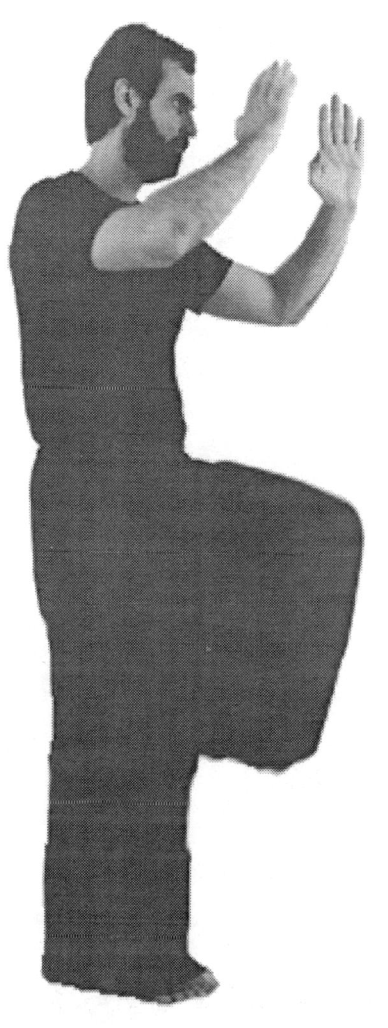

Separate the hands and raise the left knee.

The largest tree began as a tiny seed; the tallest building arose from a single stone. A journey of a thousand miles began with a single step.

39 SINGLE WHIP

Wait to shift forward.

Excess Qi can then be transmuted into Shen.

377 KICK LEFT FOOT

Shift forward and cross the arms.

64
That which is still is easy grasped. That which is fragile is easily broken. That which is small is easily scattered. It is easy to stop that which has not yet arrived. An ounce of prevention is worth a pound of cure.

40 SINGLE WHIP

Now shift and push with the left hand.

Shen can then exist beyond the limits of the body.

376 KICK LEFT FOOT

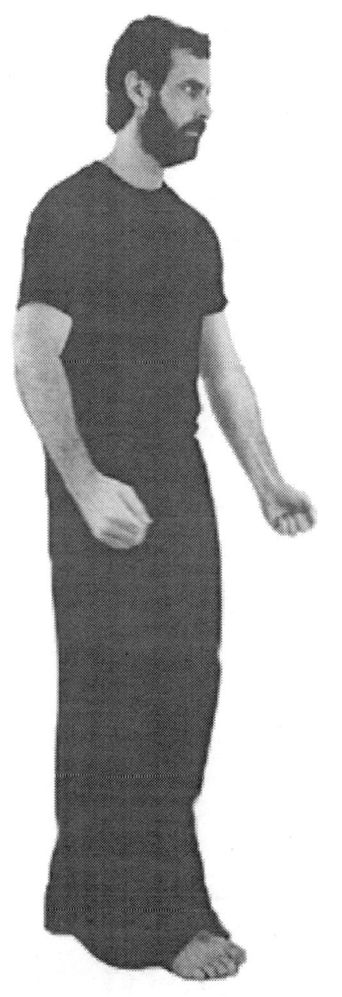

Begin to shift forward. Keep circling the hands inward.

All difficult things arose from a time when they were easy, all great things arose from small things. The sage anticipates this and acting on the small achieves the great.

41 PLAY THE HARP

375 KICK LEFT FOOT

Turn the right foot a little out.

63

The way of the Dao is to act without acting, to see what is small and few as great and many, and to repay evil with kindness. The sage will see difficulty in what seems easy and so avoid difficulties.

42 PLAY THE HARP

Bring the left hand in first, then the right foot with the right hand.

Shen is like an aura or a soul. It contains the immortal part of us.

374 KICK LEFT FOOT

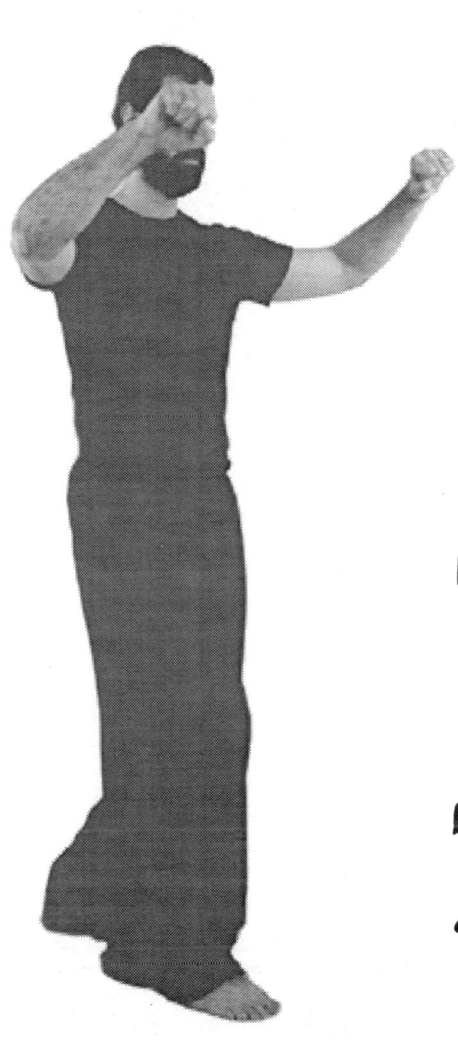

Shift backward and separate the hands back the way they came.

To a new king a humbly offered lesson in the Dao is more precious than a golden crown. The wise value the Dao because if sought it will be found and the guilty will be purified.

43 PLAY THE HARP

The right heel only lightly touches the ground. The right toes are up, all the weight is on your left leg.

Through an awareness of the symbolism and the cultivation of Qi, Tai Chi can become a spiritual practice.

373 WIND STRIKES EARS

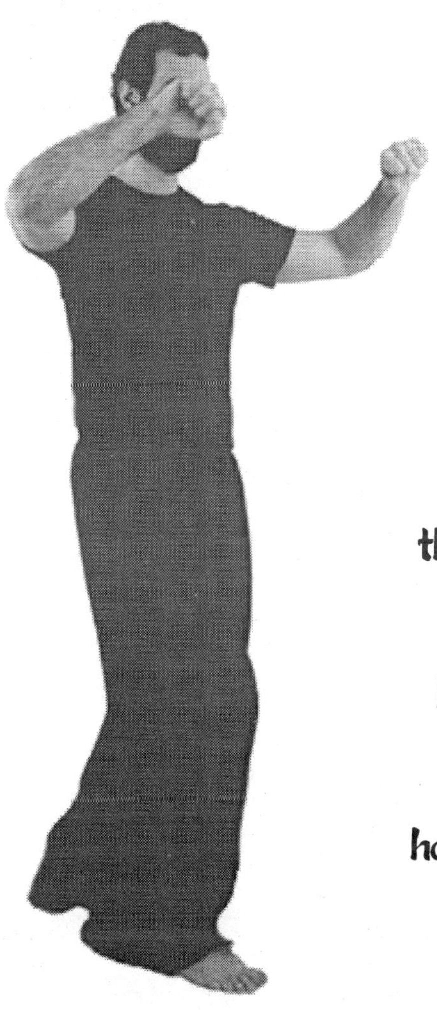

Bring the fist up to ear height.

62

The Dao is the greatest of all things. It raises the good man high and can save the bad man from himself. In the Dao good words and deeds can buy honor and bad men can find redemption.

44 PLAY THE HARP

Begin to lift the right foot as you strum the harp.

Tai Chi practiced as only physical movement is Tai Chi in the earth stage.

372 WIND STRIKES EARS

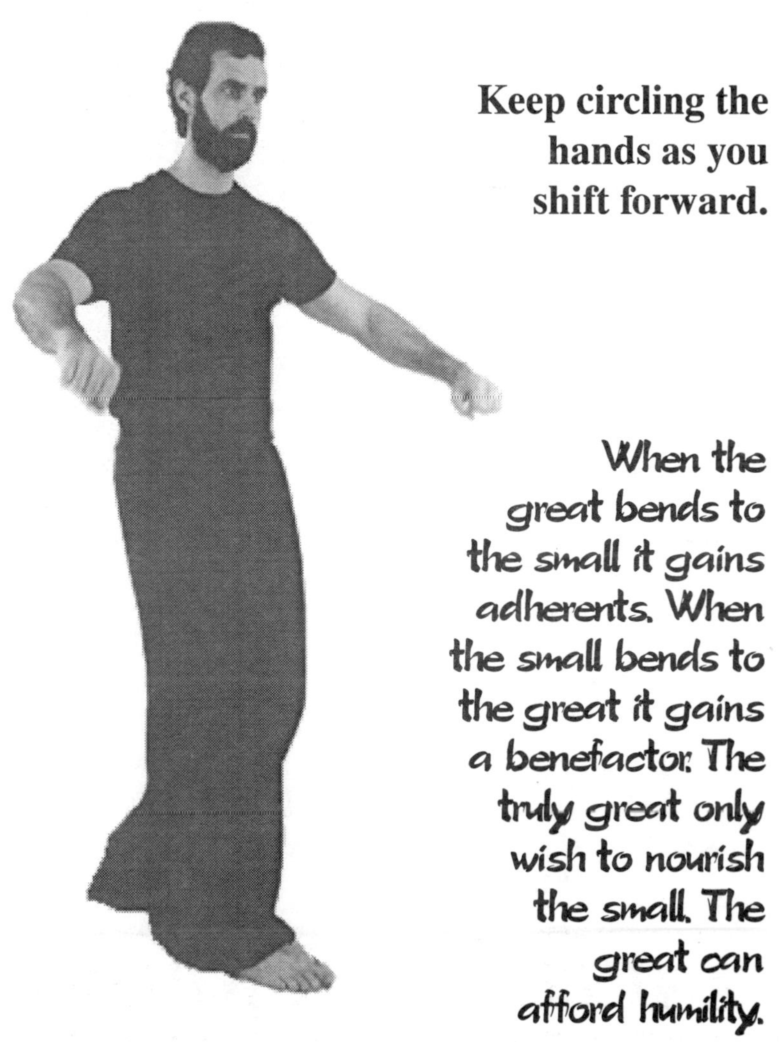

Keep circling the hands as you shift forward.

When the great bends to the small it gains adherents. When the small bends to the great it gains a benefactor. The truly great only wish to nourish the small. The great can afford humility.

45 SHOULDER STRIKE

Relax to keep good balance. Let the left leg be bent. Raise the leg only as high as is comfortable.

Tai Chi practiced with Qi is Tai Chi in the human stage.

371 WIND STRIKES EARS

Drop the hands and then circle them both up and out.

61

What makes a nation great is its willingness to practice humility. Like a low-lying river it is the center to which all the smaller streams flow. Like the male it is drawn to the female's tranquility.

46 SHOULDER STRIKE

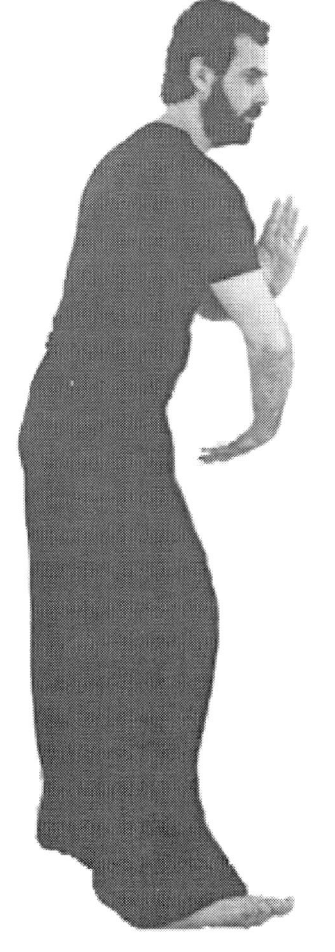

Lean very slightly into the right shoulder. Brace the right elbow with the left palm.

Tai Chi practiced with the mind is Tai Chi in the heaven stage.

370 WIND STRIKES EARS

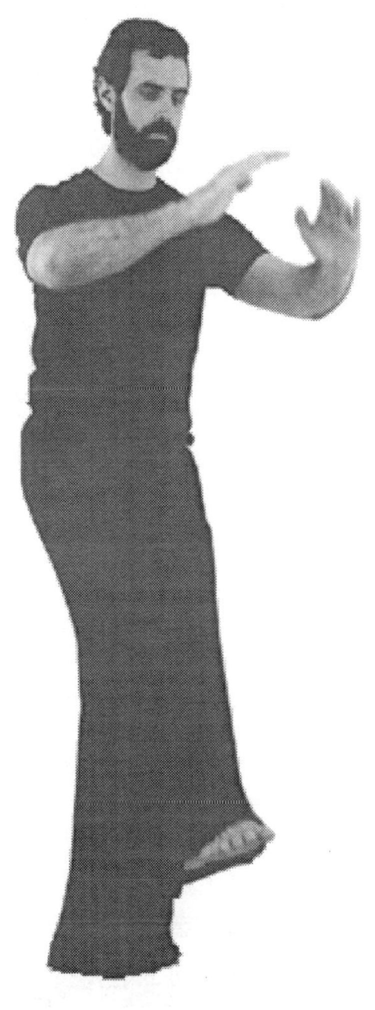

Step forward and bring the hands together like a clap.

Even though bad influences may linger, the sage will turn them to the best advantage. When the past and the present are harmonized their good influences emerge and radiate.

47 WHITE CRANE

Begin to bring the left leg forward. Start to separate the hands high and low.

As you first learn Tai Chi you will want to dwell on having proper form, a solid root and good posture.

369 WIND STRIKES EARS

Pivot on the left heel a quarter turn.

60

Governing a great nation is like cooking a small fish: too much handling ruins it. Govern according to the Dao and you will not betray the good works of your ancestors.

48 WHITE CRANE

Keep all the weight on the right foot. Only the tips of the left toes touch the earth.

As you progress you will learn to relax, breathe deeply and feel your Qi.

368 KICK RIGHT FOOT

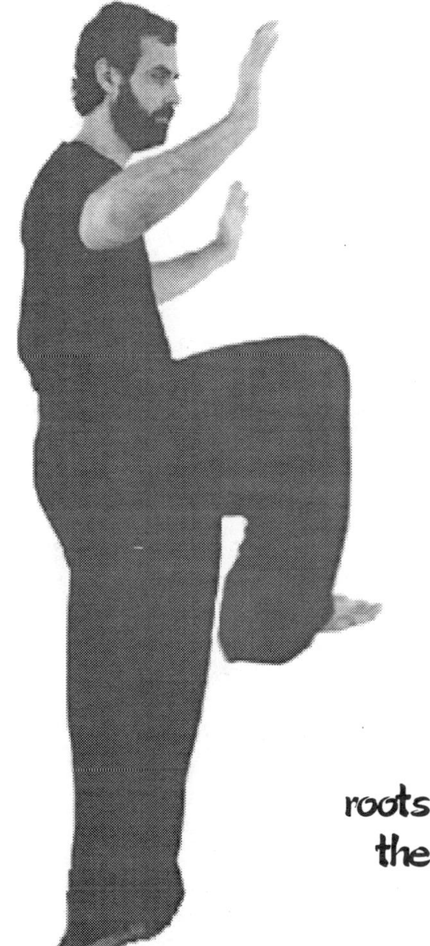

Recoil the foot.

One without limits may lead others to his vision. One with the Dao will govern long. Like a plant with deep roots and strong stalks the flower will be seen far and wide.

49 WHITE CRANE

The legs remain as in the prior movement; only your hands and waist move.

An advanced player of Tai Chi will have learned to be soft and to direct the movements and Qi with the mind.

367 KICK RIGHT FOOT

Kick with the heel.

59

Moderation is the key to governing well. Through moderation you can accumulate a reserve of the characteristics of the Dao. With this reserve you can overcome all limitations.

50 BRUSH KNEE

The hands will continue to circle, left hand clockwise, right hand counter clockwise.

Everything can be thought of in terms of Yin and Yang.

366 KICK RIGHT FOOT

Separate the hands and lift the right knee.

By trying to help we only harm. The sage is sharp and clearly defined yet cuts no one. He is a guiding light that does not bewilder.

51 BRUSH KNEE

Now step down and begin to shift forward. Your hands have continued to circle.

Wu Chi is Yin in its function as nothingness. It is Yang in its potential to create.

365 KICK RIGHT FOOT

Begin to cross the arms.

58

Trying to fix something is the quickest way to break it. Happiness is founded on tragedy. Tragedy underlies happiness. Who knows where one begins and the other ends?

52 BRUSH KNEE

The left hand has travelled just past your knee; the right hand pushes forward.

When Wu Chi and Tai Chi relate to each other, Wu Chi is Yin and Tai Chi is Yang.

364 KICK RIGHT FOOT

Shift to the left foot and drop the fists.

The sage does nothing and lets nature find its balance. He implements no plans for others and lets them find their own prosperity.

53 PLAY THE GUITAR

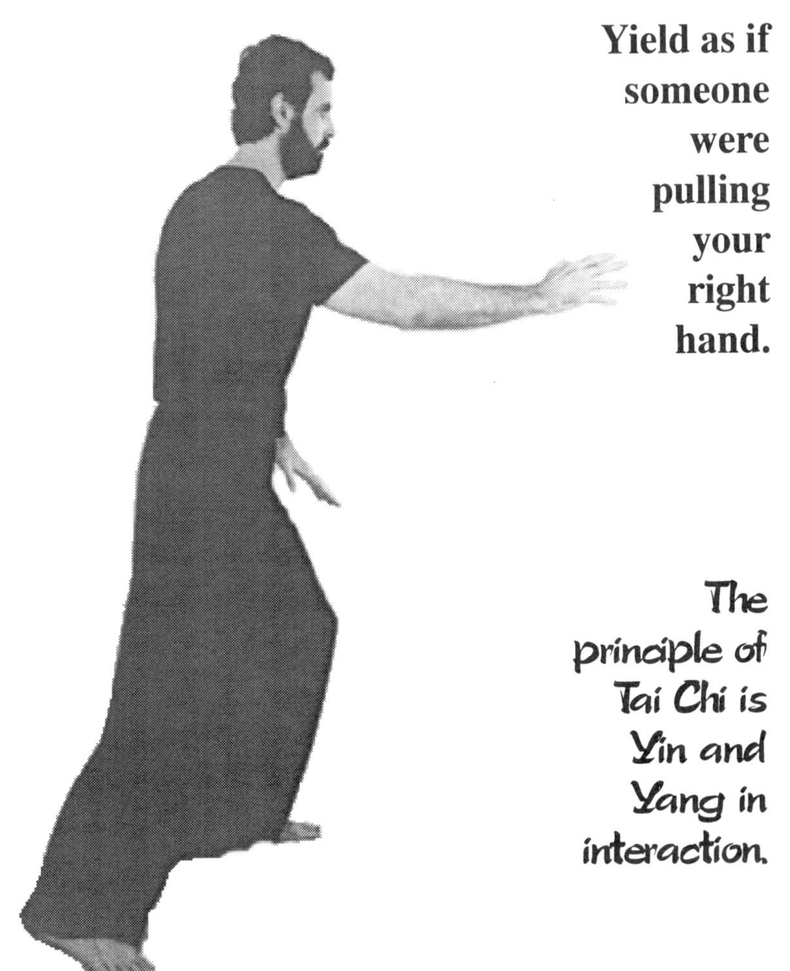

Yield as if someone were pulling your right hand.

The principle of Tai Chi is Yin and Yang in interaction.

363 HIT TIGER

Begin to shift the weight to the left foot.

57

Only through non-interference can balance be maintained. More laws make more criminals. More charity makes more need. More complexity makes more contrivance.

54 PLAY THE GUITAR

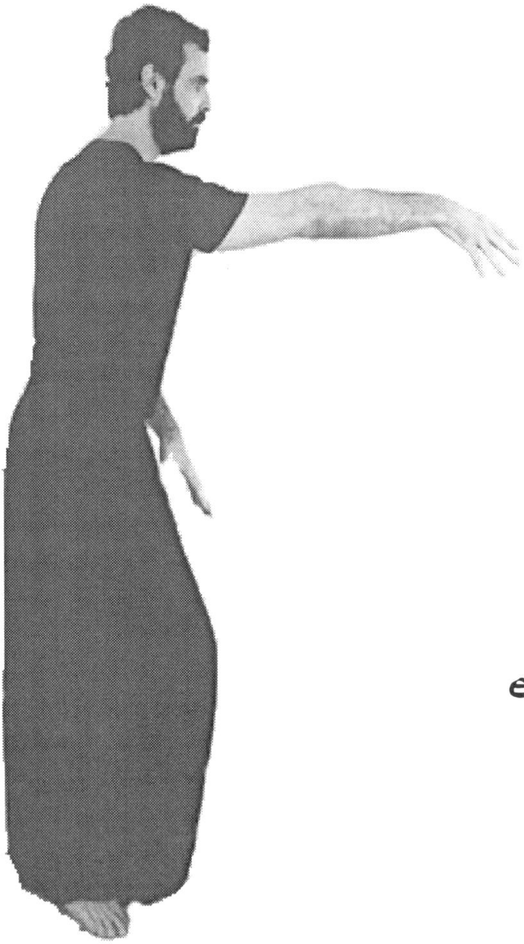

Bring the right heel to the left heel.

Earth and heaven in relation to each other are Yin to Yang.

362 HIT TIGER RIGHT

Shift forward and strike with both fists.

The sage will dovetail his ideas to the ideas of others. Such a one cannot be harmed or categorized; he is beyond the pettiness of his own ego.

55 PLAY THE GUITAR

Step back again with the right foot and a little to your right.

Earth has both Yin and Yang aspects.

361 HIT TIGER RIGHT

Step forward and bring the fists up.

56

One who knows does not need to speak. Those who speak do not know. One who knows the Dao will blunt his sharp edges and create simplicity out of complexity.

56 PLAY THE GUITAR

Circle your arms and shift back.

Yin earth is passivity. Yang earth is solidity.

360 HIT TIGER RIGHT

Shift to the left foot.

Those who know harmony have great knowledge and wisdom. To try to become stronger is to begin to die. Strength is contrary to the Dao and nothing can stand before the Dao.

57 PLAY THE GUITAR

Just the heel touches.

Yin heaven is intangibility. Yang heaven is permanence.

359 HIT TIGER RIGHT

Turn the left foot in and swing the arms across the body.

55

One who has the virtues of the Dao is like an infant. Bees will not sting him, beasts will not bite him. Though his bones are weak and his sinews soft his grip is strong.

58 PLAY THE GUITAR

Circle your arms and begin to lift your left foot.

Human Yin is in the ability to accept. Human Yang is in the ability to adapt.

358 HIT TIGER RIGHT

Shift to the right foot.

When the Dao is within yourself you will always have the truth. Put Dao in the family and the family prospers; put Dao in the community and the community thrives. Merely observe and you will see the truth of this.

59 BRUSH KNEE

Lift the leg only as high as is comfortable.

Even Yin and Yang have a Yin and Yang aspect.

357 HIT TIGER RIGHT

Open the hands and push down.

54

Whatever is planted in the Dao cannot be uprooted. Whoever follows the Dao will never become lost and his descendants will always honor him.

60 BRUSH KNEE

Step forward and out.

If darkness is
Yin, then the Yin
aspect of
darkness is the
lack of light.
The Yang
aspect
of
darkness
is its
ability to
accept light.

356 HIT TIGER LEFT

Strike high and low in the same direction.

When the outer yards are well tended the fields will be barren; where there is great wealth there is great want. This is robbery and arrogance and is against the Dao.

61 BRUSH KNEE

Keep your arms rounded and do not extend past your knee.

If the light from a candle is Yang then its brightness is its Yang aspect. The fact that the candle will burn out is its Yin aspect.

355 HIT TIGER LEFT

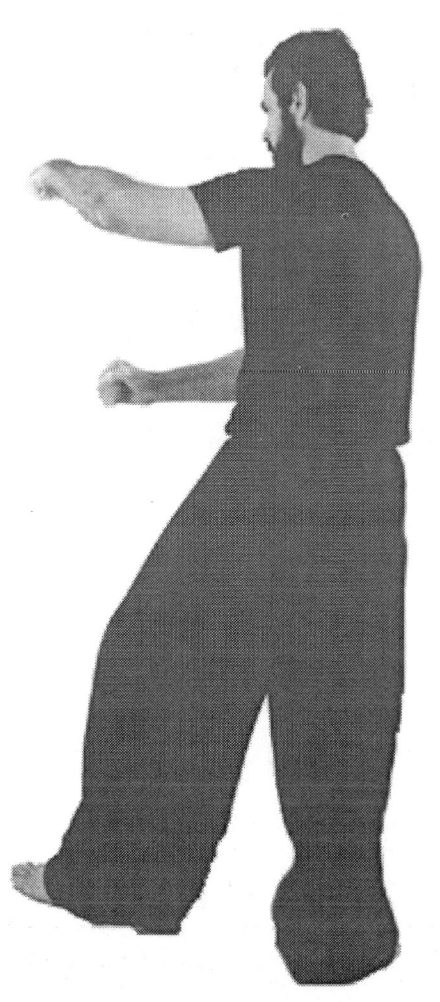

Step out and circle the fists to the right.

53

Be most afraid of arrogant display. The Dao is easy to follow but people love shortcuts.

62 BRUSH KNEE

The left hand pulls and the right hand pushes: Yin and Yang in harmony.

A straight line represents Yang.

———

A broken line is Yin.

— —

354 HIT TIGER LEFT

Make fists with both hands and begin to step out.

If you try to become strong weakness will always threaten you. If you practice softness life will be effortless. To illuminate the difference be your own light and move to the source of the light.

63 BRUSH KNEE

Shift back to turn your foot out; bring your hands with you.

The four symbols graghically illustrate the Yin and Yang aspect of Yin and Yang.

353 HIT TIGER LEFT

Swing the arms across the body to the left.

52

The Dao is the mother of all. If we know the mother we know what her children can be. If you know who your mother is you may claim your inheritance.

64 BRUSH KNEE

The left hand swings back and circles up. The right hand moves toward the ear.

The four symbols are:

Great Yang ⚌

Great Yin ⚏

Lesser Yang ⚎

Lesser Yin ⚍

352 HIT TIGER LEFT

Shift the weight to the right; keep your arms rounded.

The Dao produces all things and yet does not own them. It nourishes all things and yet expects no reward. It brings things to their fullest and allows them complete freedom.

65 BRUSH KNEE

Step forward and begin to push with the left hand.

The four symbols mated to heaven man earth give birth to the eight trigrams called Ba Gua.

351 HIT TIGER LEFT

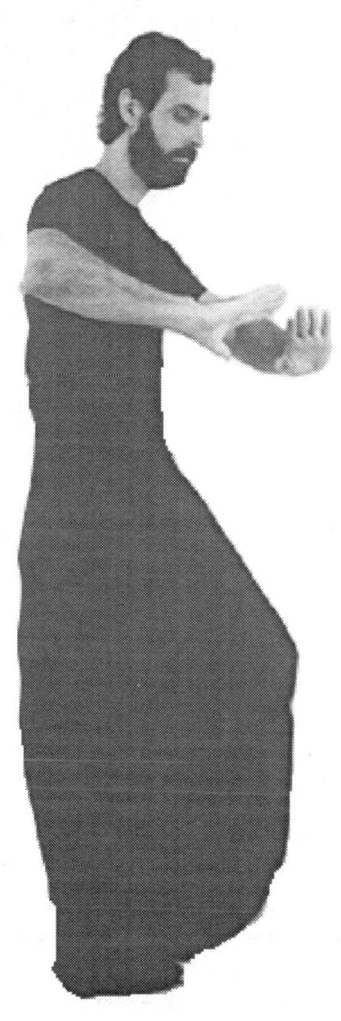

Set the right foot down with the toes turned in and push down with the hands.

51

All things come from and are nourished by the Dao. It births them and shapes them. These things are then in themselves a tribute to the Dao.

66 BRUSH KNEE

Shift forward, pull and push with the hands.

The Ba Gua are

heaven ☰

lake ☱

fire ☲

thunder ☳

wind ☴

water ☵

mountain ☶

earth ☷

350 KICK RIGHT FOOT

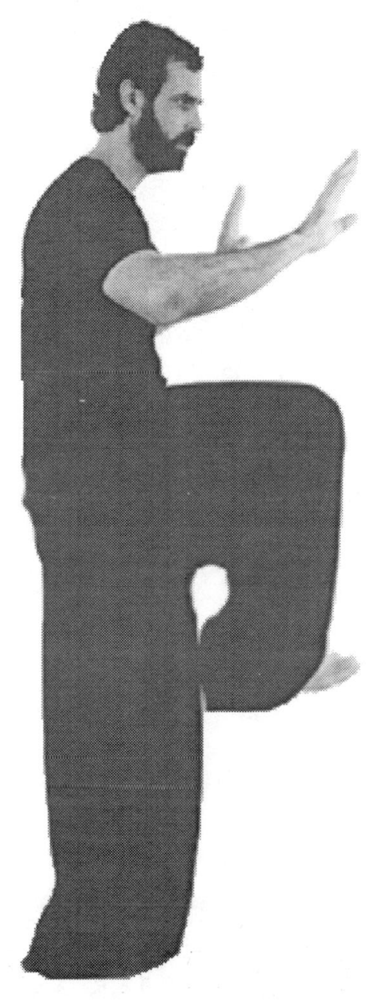

Recoil the foot and begin to bring the hands to the right.

One who embodies life can walk among tigers and swords without harm because there is no place of death in him.

67 BRUSH KNEE

Brush knee and strike with palm is the posture's full name and function.

The top line of a trigram represents heaven. The bottom line earth. The middle line humanity.

349 KICK RIGHT FOOT

Kick with the heel as high as is comfortable.

50

People live, then die. Some nurture, some destroy. Some try to produce life but instead by too much action create only death.

68 BRUSH KNEE

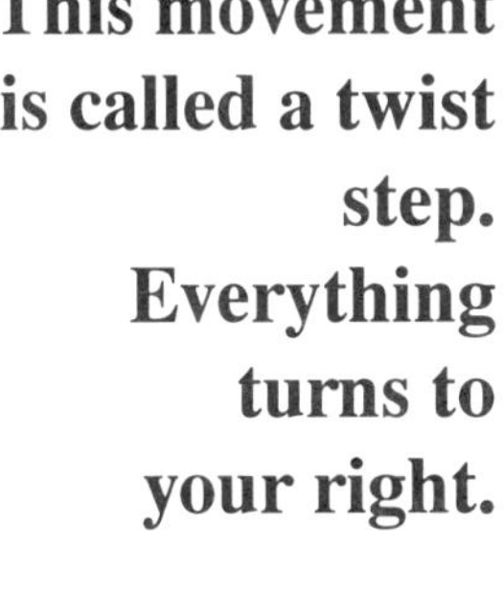

This movement is called a twist step. Everything turns to your right.

☰

This trigram represents heaven, strength, the father, creativity and the head.

348 KICK RIGHT FOOT

Stretch out the arms, but not too far.

The sage gives truth for truth and truth for falsehood. Then all have the truth. The sage is open and flexible. People respond to him as to a loving parent.

69 BRUSH KNEE

Begin to step forward as your right hand circles up.

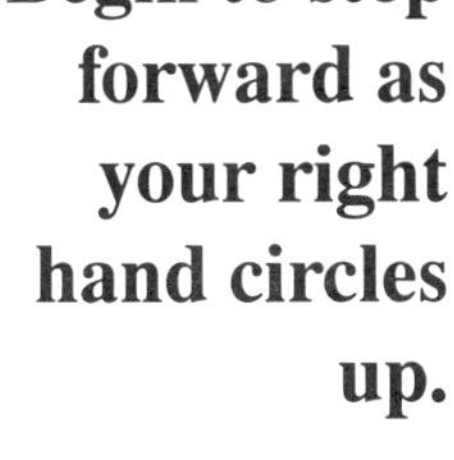

This trigram represents earth, yielding, receptivity, the mother and the belly.

347 KICK RIGHT FOOT

Begin to separate the hands and kick.

49

The sage has no inflexible mind of his own. He harmonizes with the mind of the people. He repays kindness with kindness and evil with kindness. Then all get to be kind.

70 BRUSH KNEE

Remember to step heel to toe and a little to the outside.

☱

This trigram represents lake, joy, pleasure, youngest daughter and the mouth.

346 KICK RIGHT FOOT

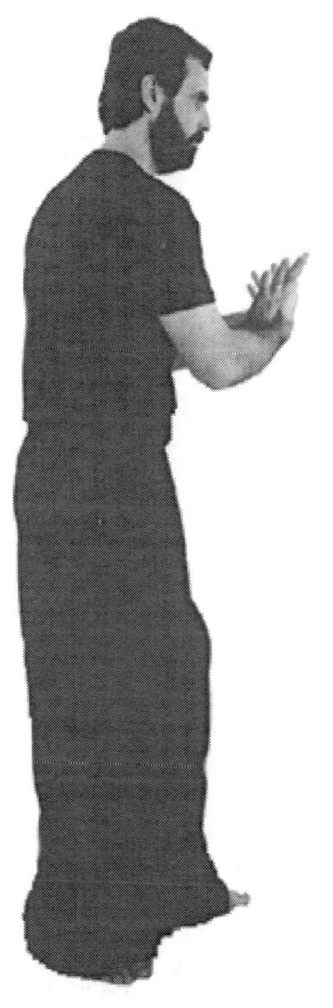

Pick up the right foot and lift the arms.

Meddling and grasping for things is the surest way to lose them. To acquire the whole world, yield to it.

71 BRUSH KNEE

Breathe out as you shift forward. One hand is Yin, one hand is Yang. One leg is Yin, one leg is Yang.

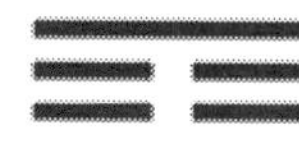

This trigram represents mountain, stillness, resting, youngest son and the hand.

345 KICK RIGHT FOOT

Cross the arms and turn the left foot out as you shift backward.

48
Those devoted to learning daily try to increase their knowledge.
Those devoted to the Dao daily decrease their doing.
Finally doing nothing there is nothing left undone.

72 BRUSH KNEE

Brush knee and strike with palm. Keep the hand very relaxed.

☲

This trigram represents fire, brightness, the sun, middle daughter and the eye.

344 PARRY AND PUNCH

Follow through.

The sage obtains
wisdom without
travelling,
understands
without
knowing,
succeeds
without trying.

73 PLAY THE GUITAR

Yield with the entire body but root powerfully on the left foot.

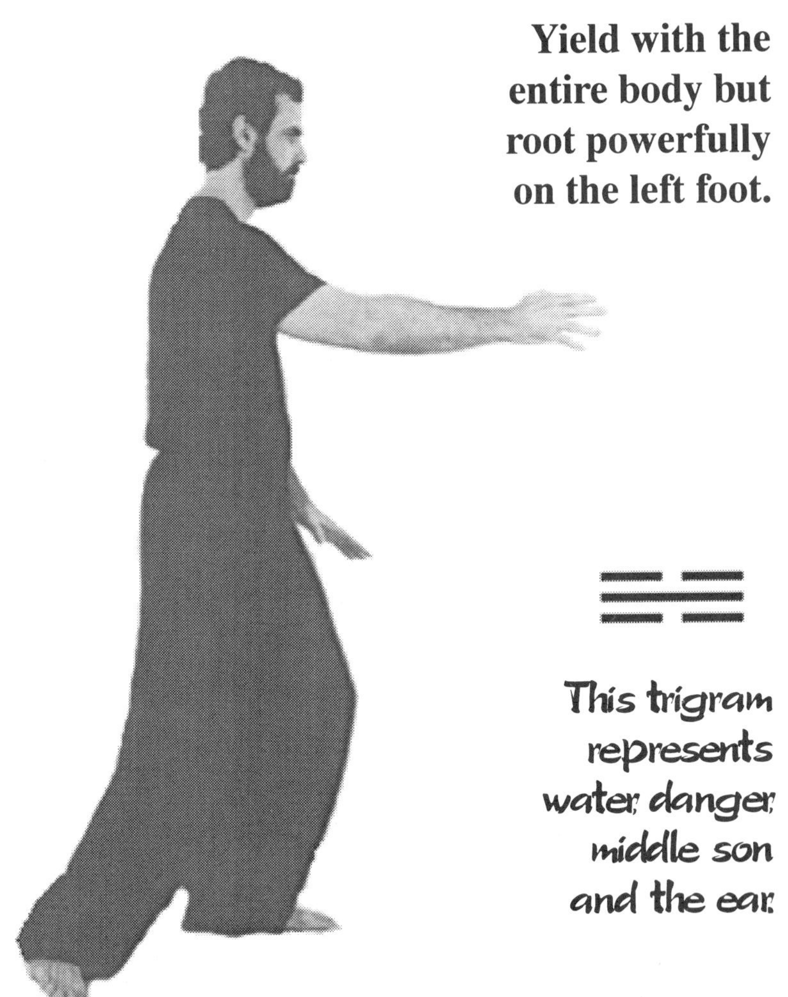

This trigram represents water, danger, middle son and the ear.

343 PARRY AND PUNCH

Bring the left hand in to touch the right forearm.

47

Without leaving his house, the sage comprehends the whole world. Without looking out his window, he sees the Dao. The farther away from yourself you travel, the less you know.

74 PLAY THE GUITAR

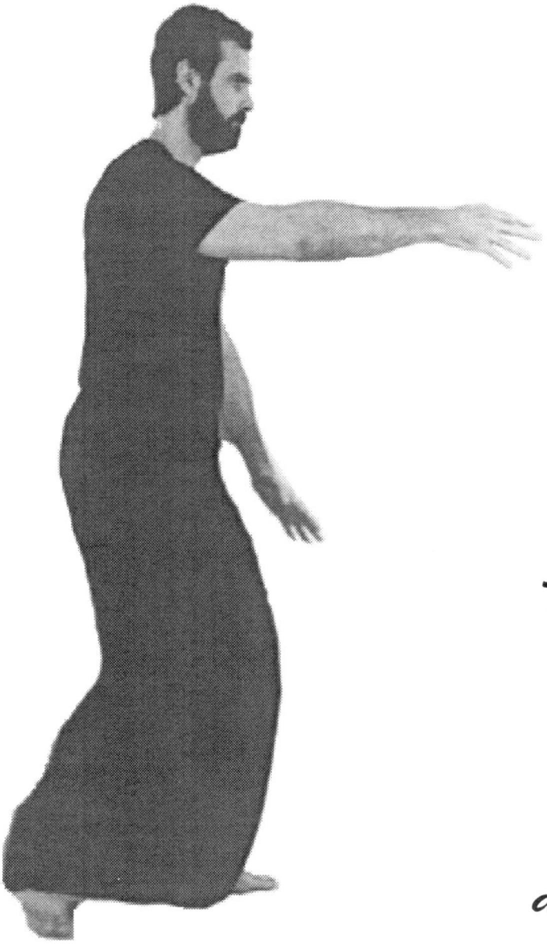

Place your feet heel to heel, shift back and begin to withdraw the arm.

☳

This trigram represents thunder, movement, arousal, eldest son and the foot.

342 PARRY AND PUNCH

Begin to shift forward and punch.

Ambition and greed create disaster. Be content to find joy in everyday life and your joy will be permanent and stable.

75 PLAY THE GUITAR

Reposition the left foot touching only the heel lightly to the floor.

This trigram represents wind, gentleness, penetration, eldest daughter and the thigh.

341 PARRY AND PUNCH

Overextend the left arm as you step forward.

46
When the Dao
is prevalent
swords are
beaten into
plowshares.
When the
Dao is
forgotten
destruction
replaces
growth.

76 PLAY THE GUITAR

Actually this posture is called play the pi-pa.

The eight trigrams correspond to the eight gates of the Tai Chi form.

340 PARRY AND PUNCH

Shift forward and poke with the fingers.

Activity conquers cold. Stillness subdues heat. Activity and stillness balance all the things of the universe.

77 PLAY THE GUITAR

This is the opposite posture of play the harp.

The eight gates refer to eight concepts of strategy, movements of the arm and actual postures.

339 PARRY AND PUNCH

Set the heel down first and bring the hands across the body.

45

Long-lasting achievements seem poor at first. Wholeness seems incomplete. Great art is artless and true speech seems false.

78 BRUSH KNEE

Cycle the hands around and lift the leg as high as is comfortable.

The eight gates are: ward off, roll back, press, push, pull, split, elbow and shoulder.

338 PARRY AND PUNCH

Bring the hands up and across your face; turn the right toes out.

Be content with what you already have; celebrate ordinary life. If you trust in the everyday you will have no regrets.

79 BRUSH KNEE

Almost like a kick, step the leg forward and out with a circular swinging motion.

Ward off, roll back, press and push are called the four directions.

337 ROLL BACK

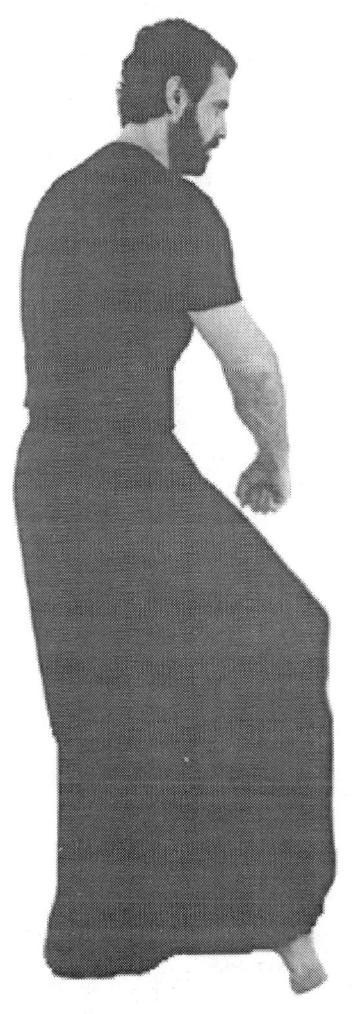

Let the hands drop a little as you pick up your right foot.

44

Which is more valuable, fame or life? Which is more precious, life or riches? Cultivate life, not superficiality.

80 BRUSH KNEE

Step heel to toe and wait to shift.

Pull, split, elbow and shoulder are called the four corners.

336 ROLL BACK

Roll back and strike with the fist as one movement.

There are few indeed who can teach without words and accomplish without acting. It is the challenge of the sage.

81 BRUSH KNEE

Keep your back straight and do not overextend.

The four directions imply the use of straight-line movement. The four corners imply the use of angles.

335 ROLL BACK

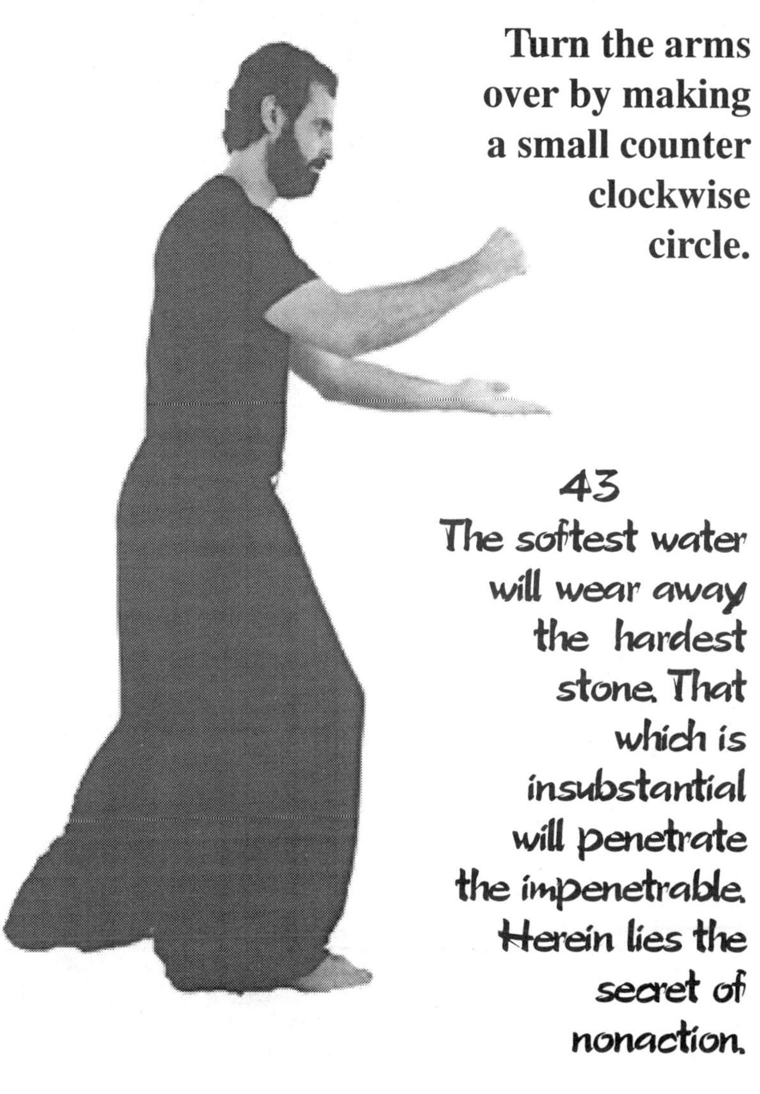

Turn the arms over by making a small counter clockwise circle.

43
The softest water will wear away the hardest stone. That which is insubstantial will penetrate the impenetrable. Herein lies the secret of nonaction.

82 BRUSH KNEE

Your hands move forward only as far as the knee.

Ward off refers to the basic roundness of the arm and is the basis for all the arm movements.

334 TURN AND CHOP

Pull the fist back and poke the fingers forward.

Loss can engender gain; gain can engender loss. What others teach is taught again here. The violent and strong do not die a natural death.

83 DEFLECT DOWN

Shift back and turn your left foot out to the side.

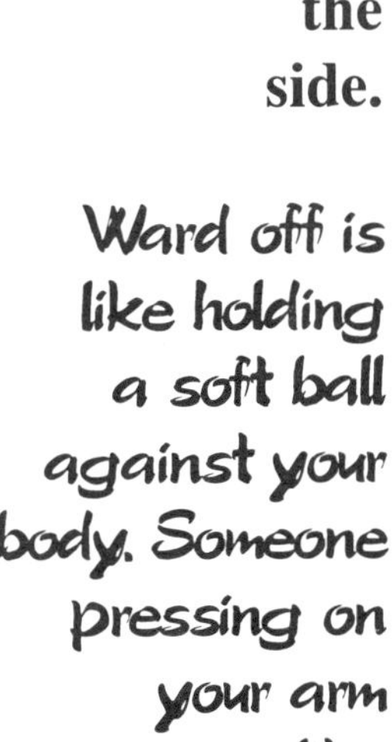

Ward off is like holding a soft ball against your body. Someone pressing on your arm is like a boat floating on the water.

333 TURN AND CHOP

Begin to shift forward.

42

The Dao gave birth to one, One produced two, two produced three and from three came all things. All things emerge from void and move into being. When void and being are merged harmony is created.

84 DEFLECT DOWN

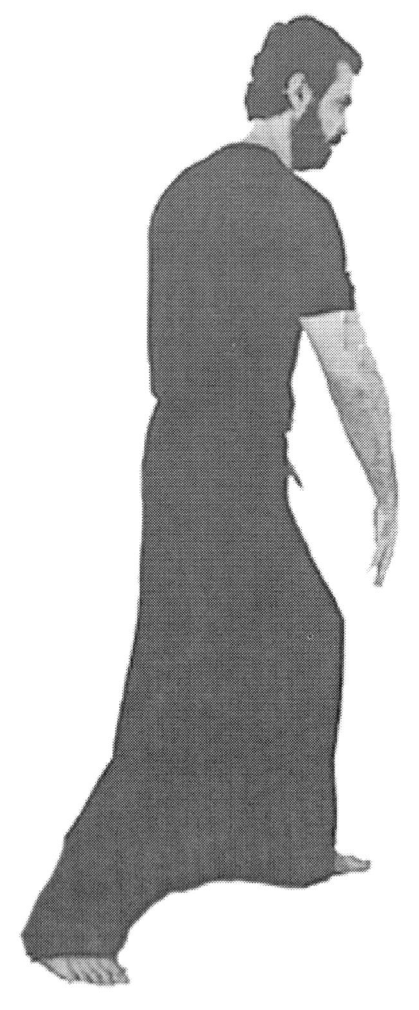

Imagine you are brushing a kick away from your stomach.

The ward-off arm is uncollapsible through the resiliency of the waist and legs, not through rigidity of the arm.

332 TURN AND CHOP

Step forward and out.

It is said that the Dao's brightest light seems dim, its easiest path seems steep, its firmest truth is mutable. The Dao is hidden and quiet but does everything.

85 PARRY AND PUNCH

Pick up the right foot by lifting the knee.

All arm positions can be thought of as variations of ward off. Ward off is the idea of using the arm as a part of the waist.

331 TURN AND CHOP

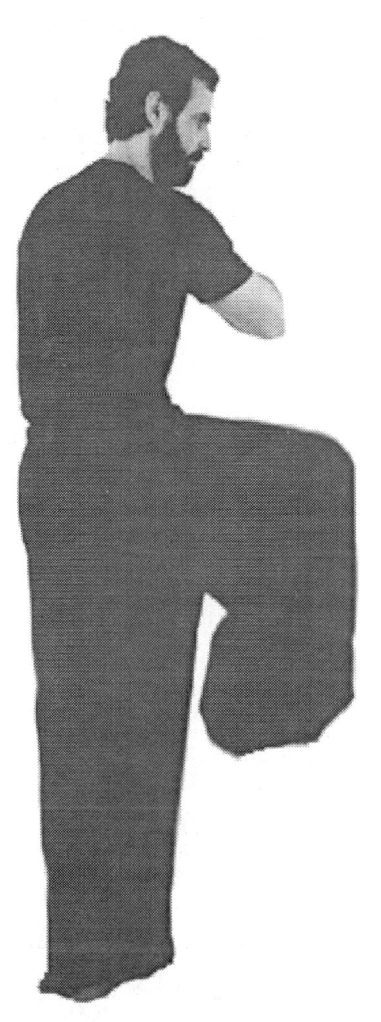

Keep circling the arms. The right fist is by the chest. The left hand is near the left hip.

41

When a superior person learns of the Dao he puts it into practice. When an average person learns of the Dao he uses it off and on. When a fool learns of it he laughs. If he did not laugh it would not be the Dao.

86 PARRY AND PUNCH

The right hand makes a loose fist. The right foot turns out.

The ward off arm begins at the breast bone and spine and reaches all the way to the fingertips. Imagine you have no shoulder.

330 TURN AND CHOP

Shift to the left foot. Circle the left hand out and back in a large arc. Circle the right fist upward.

All things spring from the Dao of existence. Existence springs from the Dao of nonexistence. One creates two, zero creates one.

87 PARRY AND PUNCH

Set your heel down with your toes still turned out. The fist and hand swing past your chest.

Ward off corresponds to the trigram heaven.

☰

329 TURN AND CHOP

Your hand faces palm out. Shift to the right foot and lean slightly.

40

The Dao manifests through contraries. Through weakness it accomplishes great works.

88 PARRY AND PUNCH

Overextend your left hand. You will shift and step forward in one motion.

Roll back expresses the basic strategy of Tai Chi. When confronted with force, yield and redirect.

328 TURN AND CHOP

Bring the fist to your hip. Raise the left hand to head height. Turn in the right foot.

Greatness finds its root in smallness. The sage reveres the low for in it he sees the high.

89 PARRY AND PUNCH

Step wide with your left foot. Clear a path for your fist with your left hand.

Roll back is soft and rounded. It channels force away from you on a circular path back to its source.

327 TURN AND CHOP

Rise up smoothly; bring the fist in to the body.

39

Issuing from the Dao, heaven is clear and bright, earth is solid and fertile. Without the Dao the sky would fall and the earth would open up.

90 PARRY AND PUNCH

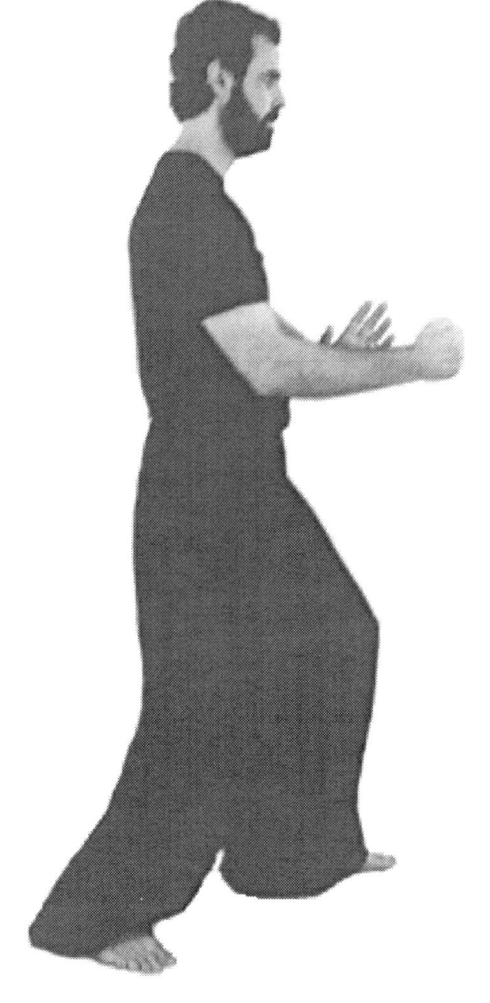

Brace the forearm of your punch with the left palm. Stay relaxed, punch with a soft pushing motion.

Roll back can be thought of as ward off in its defensive mode.

326 PUNCH DOWNWARD

Follow through with the waist.

To live with a half-truth is to court chaos. The sage abides by what is real and rejects what is false. He dwells with the fruit and not the flower.

91 WITHDRAW

Open your fist like a flower blossoming. Slide the left palm under the elbow.

Roll back is like canyon walls that channel a river. Roll back can control a thousand pounds of force with only four ounces of pressure.

325 PUNCH DOWNWARD

Brush knee and punch downward almost to the earth.

38

Those steeped in the Dao do not show it. They do not need to do anything. Most people have only a portion of the Dao and are always trying to enforce their partial truth on the world.

92 WITHDRAW

Slide the right arm over the left palm with a pulling motion.

Roll back corresponds to the trigram earth.

☷

324 PUNCH DOWNWARD

Sink as low as is comfortable; keep the feet flat.

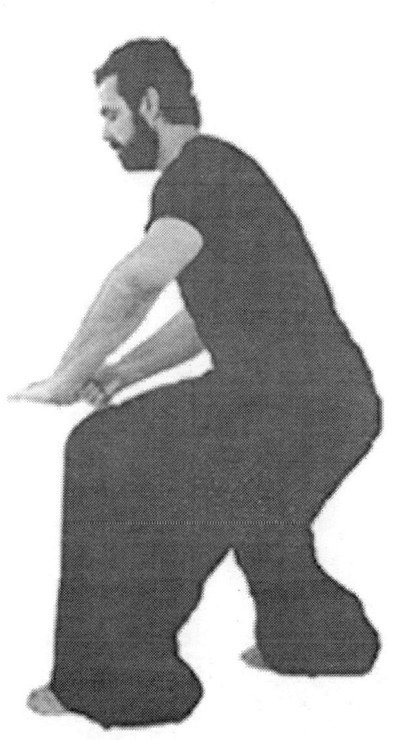

If people refrained from interfering and let go of their desires all things would dwell in blissful balance and simplicity.

93 WITHDRAW

Bring your arms slightly to the right, and begin to cycle them up.

Press is to use the back of the ward off arm to attack.

323 PUNCH DOWNWARD

Step forward, begin to brush knee while sinking lower to the ground.

37

The Dao does nothing and so there is nothing which it does not do. If kings and queens were one with the Dao the world would be transformed by itself.

94 DOUBLE PUSH

Cycle the hands around till they are in front of the face.

Press seeks the smallest of weaknesses. Like water seeping through a crack in a dam, very soon a flood will pour forth and the dam will burst.

322 TWIST STEP

Keep the left hand high and make a fist with your right hand.

Bringing that which is mysterious into the light will be the death of it. The sage does not flaunt his methods; he lets the results speak for themselves.

95 DOUBLE PUSH

Begin to shift forward. Exhale and angle the forearms upward.

Press corresponds to the trigam water.

321 TWIST STEP

Circle the right hand down.

36

Before you can inhale you must exhale. Before one can be overthrown he must be raised up. The soft overcomes the hard; the weak conquers the strong.

96 DOUBLE PUSH

Root firmly and sink the body deeply. Relax into the push.

Push is to use the ward off arm in a forehand gesture to bring power to the hand or fist.

320 TWIST STEP

Begin to shift back.

Music and
fine food
make people
take notice.
Words of the
Dao
seem boring
and useless.
Yet the uses of
the Dao are
without
number.

97 RAINBOW

Bring the left toes and both hands with you as you shift back and turn.

In double push apply energy with only one hand. The other hand is receptive. The waist can only work in one direction.

319 BRUSH KNEE

Follow through.

35
Those who
grasp the
Dao are a
great benefit
to the world.
All who come
to them
receive peace,
comfort and
balance.

98 RAINBOW

The left foot will feel slightly pigeon-toed. Your hands will follow a smooth arc.

Push begins as a spark which feeds on the available energy until all is ashes.

318 BRUSH KNEE

Shift forward.

The sage has
the way of
the Dao and
accomplishes
great things.
Only by not
making himself
great can he
achieve these
things.

99 CLOSE UP

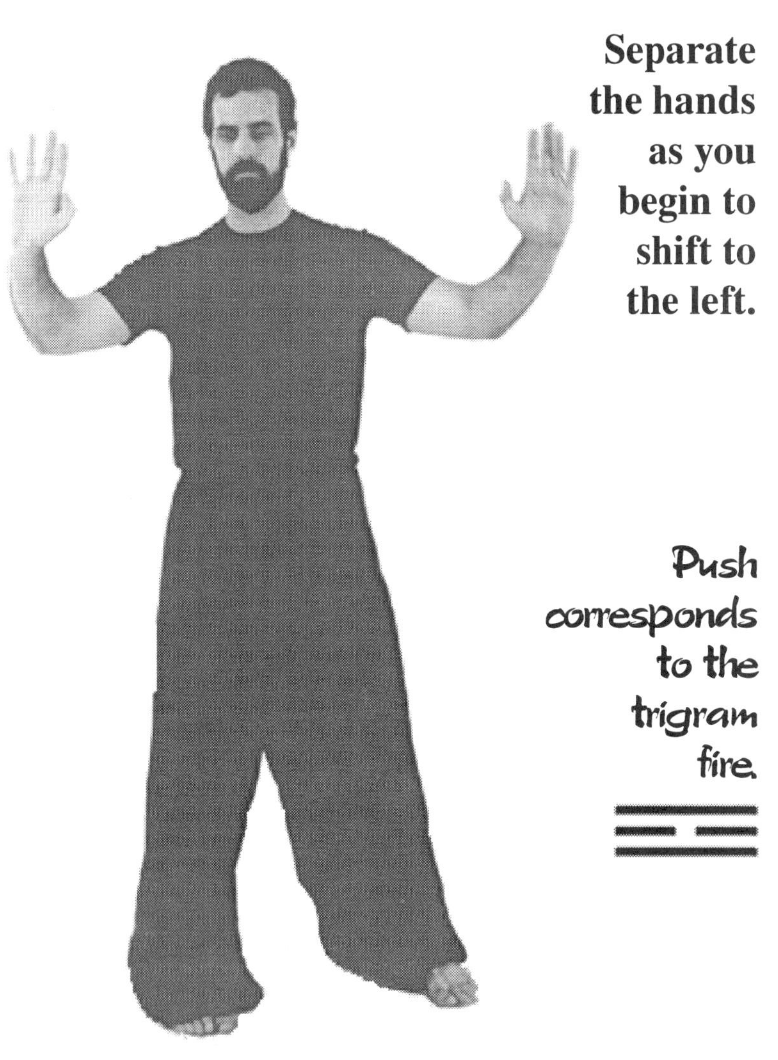

Separate the hands as you begin to shift to the left.

Push corresponds to the trigram fire.

317 BRUSH KNEE

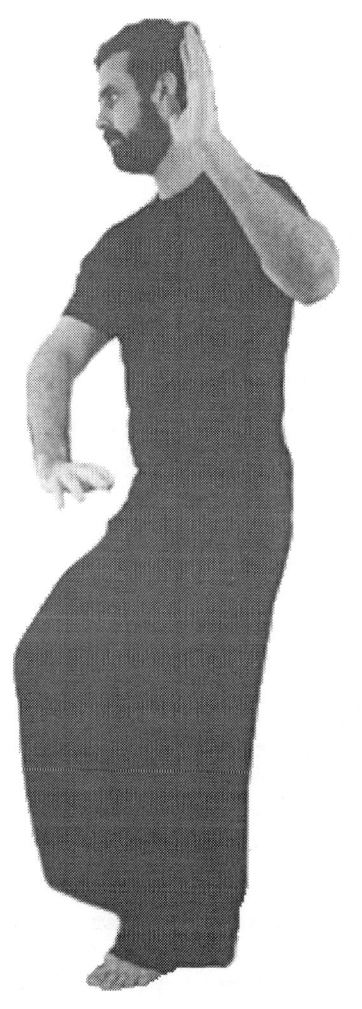

The right hand deflects away from your belly.

34

The Dao is inescapable. All things depend on it, all things bend to it, yet it claims no credit.

100 CLOSE UP

Begin to draw the right leg back.

Pull is to use roll back to attack.

316 TWIST STEP

Shift forward and begin to take a step.

Those who succeed will survive for a time. Those who know the value of loss will never perish.

101 CLOSE UP

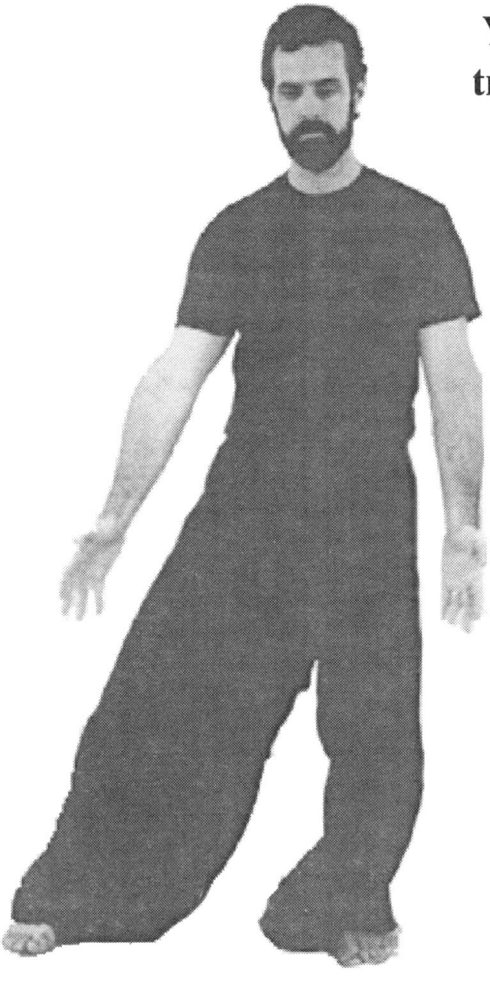

You will want to try to harmonize the right foot with the right hand.

Pull uses the ward off arm to grasp while redirecting the opponent into imbalance.

315 TWIST STEP

Turn the left toes out.

33

Knowing others is intelligence; knowing yourself is better. Conquering others is strength; conquering oneself is best.

102 CLOSE UP

Shift double-weighted as you close up. You are moving from Tai Chi to Wu Chi.

Pull is like a whirlwind that uproots a house.

314 TWIST STEP

Begin to shift backward and bring the hands to your left.

The Dao that can be seen can draw people into it. When people rest in the Dao they are free from error. The Dao is like the sea to which all waters flow.

103 CLOSE UP

This ends the first section. You can stop here if you wish by dropping the arms to your sides and rising up.

Pull corresponds to the trigram wind.

313 BRUSH KNEE

Shift forward; brush knee and strike with palm.

32

The primordial Dao that has no name is pregnant with unimaginable power. When people do not interfere, it harmonizes heaven and earth and all receive the benefits.

104 EMBRACE TIGER

Flow immediately into the next movement.

Split is when both ward off arms work in opposition.

312 BRUSH KNEE

Step forward and out. The right hand is pushing.

To the sage, engaging in violence is the same as attending a funeral. There is no joy in it.

105 EMBRACE TIGER

Begin to turn in the left foot.

The action of split is like using the arms to pedal a bicycle. The arms harmonize through the waist.

311 TURN AND KICK

Recoil the kick and bring your hands in towards your right ear.

31

Weapons are tools of death. The sage avoids them and turns to them only as a last resort. Peace he prizes most; to desire victory is to desire the harm of others.

106 EMBRACE TIGER

Begin to shift the weight to the left foot.

Split is like spinning a great wheel; anything that touches it will immediately be thrown off.

310 TURN AND KICK

Keep the foot flexed. Kick with the heel.

Strike only out of direst need and not out of a wish to dominate. To seek strength is to court death.

107 EMBRACE TIGER

Keep the hands circling and the left foot turned in.

Split
happens
like a bolt
of lightning
out of a
clear blue sky.
It surprises
everyone
and shakes
the earth

309 TURN AND KICK

Kick and separate the hands.

30
Violence reaps violence. Where violence lives, only death prospers. All who rise fall.

108 EMBRACE TIGER

You will be stepping to the rear diagonal.

Split corresponds to the trigram thunder.

☳

308 TURN AND KICK

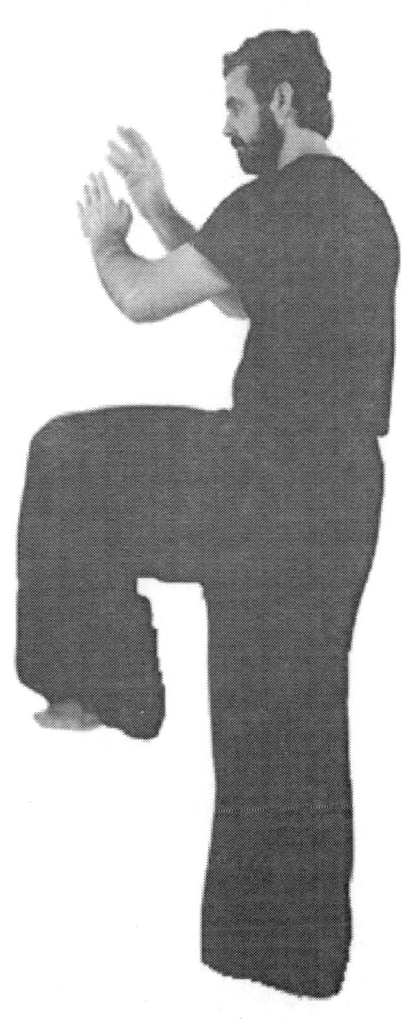

Lift the left knee and the crossed arms.

The natural process is such that what is in front will be behind, what is hot will soon be cold, what is strong will soon grow weak. The sage has patience and need only wait for what he wants.

109 EMBRACE TIGER

The movement is the same as brush knee and strike with palm.

Elbow refers to using the middle part of the ward off arm.

307 TURN AND KICK

Shift the weight to the right foot and cross the arms.

29

To take action to try to effect change is to destroy that which you would save. To try to change with action is to try to possess. The tighter you grip the more it slips away.

110 EMBRACE TIGER

The full name of the posture is embrace tiger, return to the mountain.

If the forearm collapses, the elbow immediately comes into play.

306 TURN AND KICK

Keep turning the body. Turn in the right foot.

Know glory but seek anonymity; recognize the glory in the world and you will have found the Dao. The unshaped clay has the most possible uses; the sage will refrain from diminishing these possibilities.

111 EMBRACE TIGER

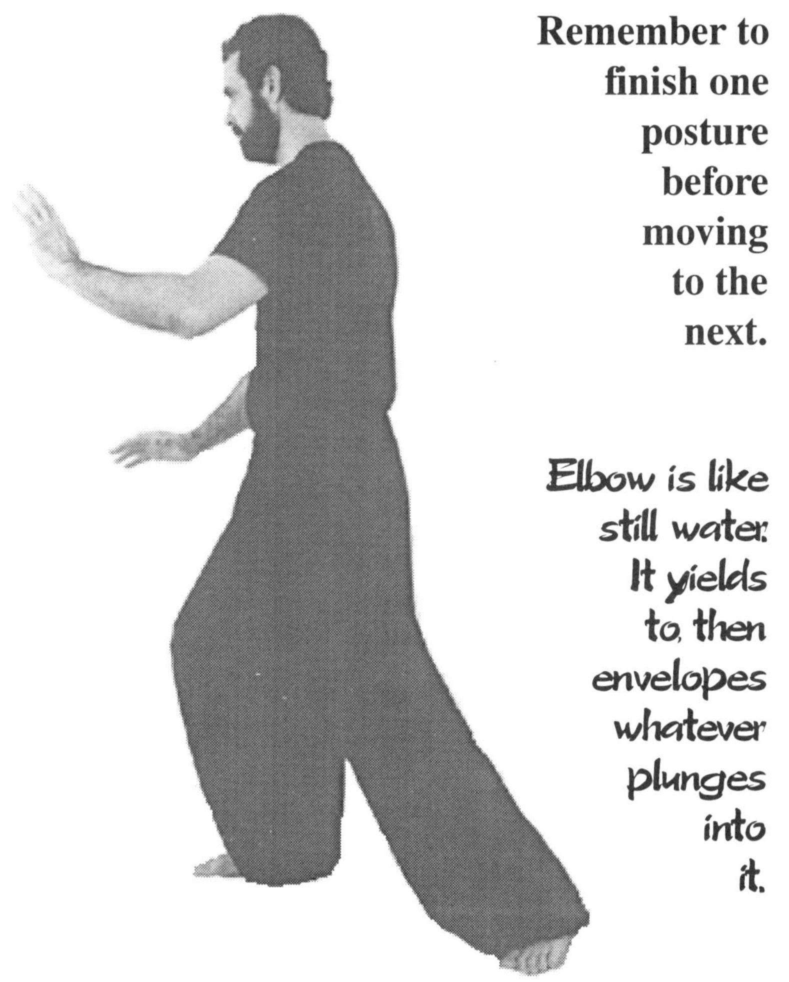

Remember to finish one posture before moving to the next.

Elbow is like still water: It yields to, then envelopes whatever plunges into it.

305 TURN AND KICK

Shift the weight to the left foot and turn while still deflecting with the hands.

28

Know your maleness
but cultivate your
femaleness; remain
simple and open
and you will
have the joy
of the child.
Know the Yang
yet keep to
the Yin; be a
reflection of the
world and you will
know the Dao.

112 ROLL BACK

Begin to shift back and cycle the arms to the left.

Elbow corresponds to the trigram lake.

☱

304 TURN AND KICK

Brush an imaginary kick away from the body.

The man of skill is the obligated teacher of those without skill. Teacher and student are involved in a dance; sometimes it is difficult to know who leads.

113 ROLL BACK

Move the body first and let the hands follow.

Shoulder refers to using the back, upper arm and shoulder part of the ward off arm.

303 TURN AND KICK

Step back with the left foot.

27

The skillful traveller
leaves no footprints;
the skillful binder
ties no knots.
The sage is
skillful at
saving men
and considers
nothing worthless.
He works inside the
Dao and so his work
cannot be undone.

114 ROLL BACK

Remember to feel the right elbow involved in the movement.

If the hand and elbow are controlled, the shoulder is the last line of defense.

302 RUB LEFT FOOT

Recoil the kick and begin to drop the hands.

If you let others move you, you will lose your root. If you lose your root, you will never have a home.

115 ROLL BACK

At the extreme of Yin in rollback you will flow into the beginning of Yang in press.

To be rooted and solid like Mount Everest is very important to shoulder.

301 RUB LEFT FOOT

Toes pointed, kick up and out.

26

Heaviness is the root of lightness, stillness the creator of movement. The sage travels without moving, is light but rooted.

116 PRESS

Lead with the waist and legs.

Shoulder corresponds to the trigram mountain.

☶

300 RUB LEFT FOOT

Kick and separate the arms.

The Dao flows in an unceasing cycle. Man follows earth, earth follows heaven, heaven follows the Dao, the Dao obeys only its own rule.

117 PRESS

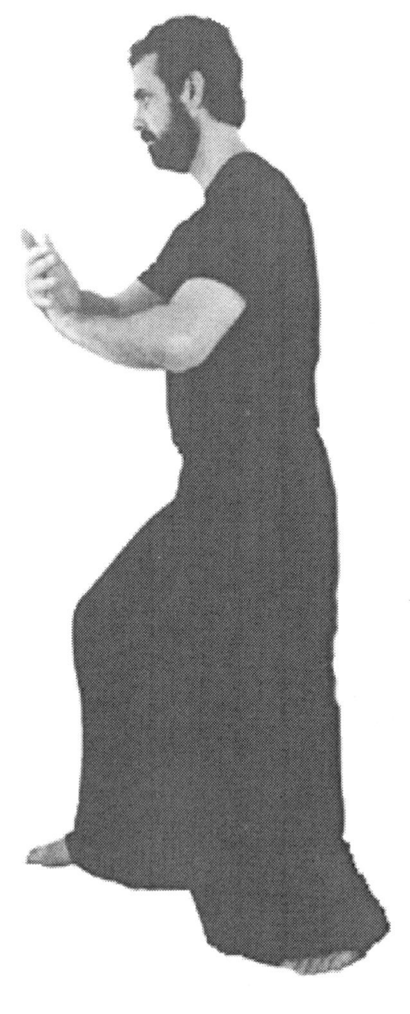

Follow through but do not overextend.

Studying the trigrams will provide clues as to the correct feel and application of the eight gates.

299 RUB LEFT FOOT

Gather up the hands and lift the knee.

25

There was something whole but unnamed before heaven and earth were created. It was still, alone, changeless and without form, infinite and inexhaustible. The mother of all. The Dao.

118 PRESS

At the extreme Yang of press, flow into the Yin of the next movement.

Practicing the eight gates will provide insight into the deeper meaning of the trigrams.

298 RUB LEFT FOOT

Shift forward and begin to lift the left foot as you keep circling the left arm.

Those who follow the Dao are without vanity. Pride is like leftover food; it is for those who have nothing else.

119 DOUBLE PUSH

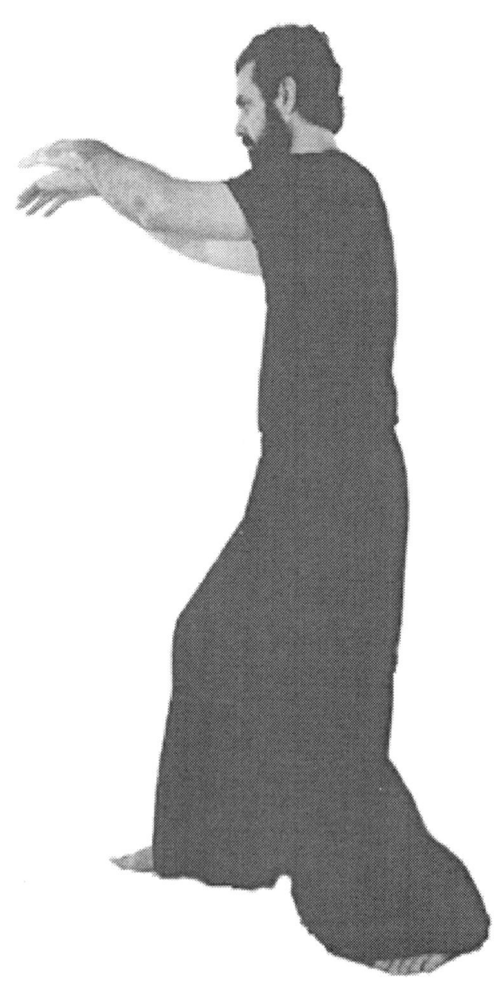

Be careful to stay low and sink the weight.

Two trigrams combined one above the other form a hexagram.

297 RUB LEFT FOOT

Turn the right toes out. Lift the right arm into a ward off position.

24

If you stand on tiptoes, you will fall. If you show conceit you will be thought inferior. If you exalt yourself you will not be acknowledged.

120 DOUBLE PUSH

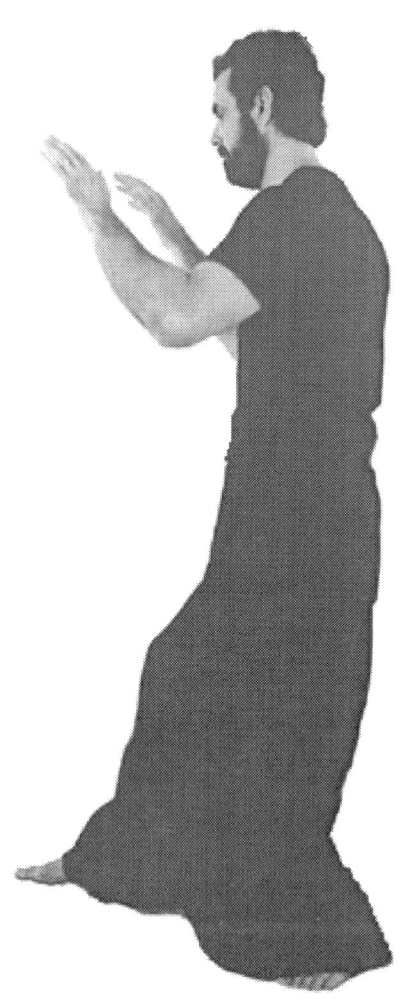

Feel as if you are getting under the push.

There are sixty-four possible combinations of trigrams into hexagrams.

296 RUB LEFT FOOT

Shift back, circle the left arm up and out.

Those who follow the Dao express only the truth. Everyone will respond to the truth and so come closer to the Dao.

121 DOUBLE PUSH

A good push will endeavor to uproot the opponent.

The sixty-four hexagrams are called the I Ching. I Ching means 'book of changes.' I means both constancy and change.

295 STACK UP

Stack the hands above the knee.

23
Refraining from speaking shows a spontaneous nature. Even heaven and earth cannot make the wind blow forever.

122 DOUBLE PUSH

Follow through without over-extending.

The top two lines of a hexagram represent heaven. The middle lines are humanity. The bottom two lines are earth.

294 STACK UP

Step forward and out to the right.

The sage's humility allows all things to come to him. Since he does not contend, no one can fight him. To understand that everything is part of a cycle is the only way to find completion.

123 FLAT RAINBOW

Begin to turn the right foot inward.

The bottom line of a hexagram is the first line. The top line is the sixth.

293 STACK UP

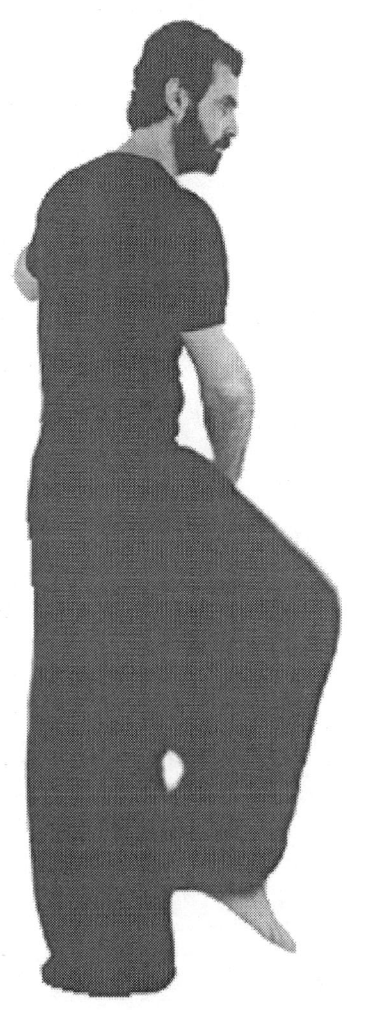

The left hand is over the right hand. The palms are facing each other.

22

The part becomes whole, the bent becomes straight, the empty is filled and the old is renewed. Want little and you will have it, want much and you will spend your whole life seeking.

124 FLAT RAINBOW

Keep the hands away from the body.

The hexagram for peace shows heaven moving into earth. It indicates spring, growth and a time of abundance.

292 RUB RIGHT FOOT

Pull in the right hand and let the kick recoil.

In the Dao everything is in flux between beginning and ending. The sage knows there is no death, only birth; there is no decay, only growth.

125 FLAT RAINBOW

Keep turning in the right foot. The weight is on the left leg.

The hexagram for stagnation shows the weak coming into the strong. It indicates retrogression, the autumn and inevitable decay.

291 RUB RIGHT FOOT

Toes pointed, kick up and to the outside. You need not kick high.

21

All things emerge from the Dao. Yet it cannot be seen or felt. The Dao is dark and unfathomable and yet all things begin and end there.

126 FLAT RAINBOW

Place the right foot down in a pigeon-toed position.

The hexagrams and trigrams provide progressive symbols that can help us to understand universal processes, ourselves, our past, present and future.

290 RUB RIGHT FOOT

Kick and separate the hands.

Most people seem to be at a banquet, busy and involved. The sage seems alone, listless and dull. But he takes his nourishment from the mother of all.

127 FLAT SINGLE WHIP

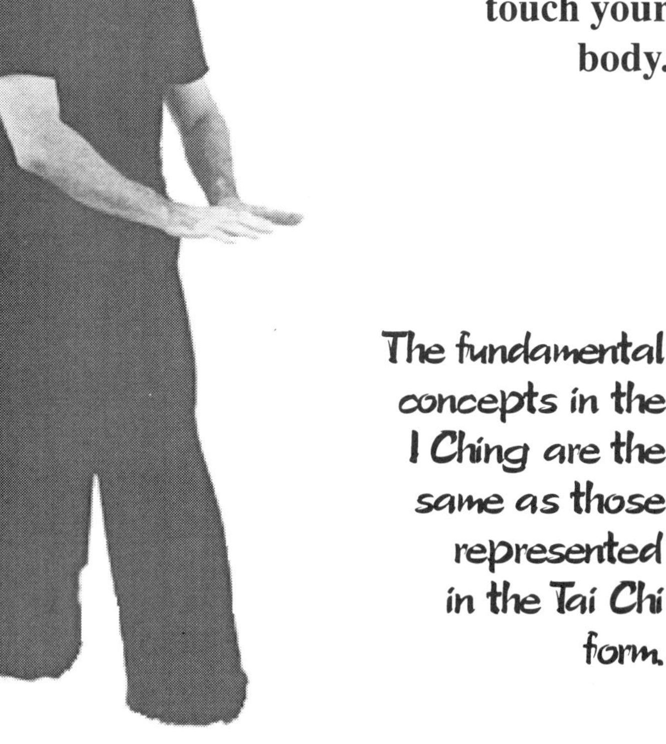

Bring the hands in until they almost touch your body.

The fundamental concepts in the I Ching are the same as those represented in the Tai Chi form.

289 RUB RIGHT FOOT

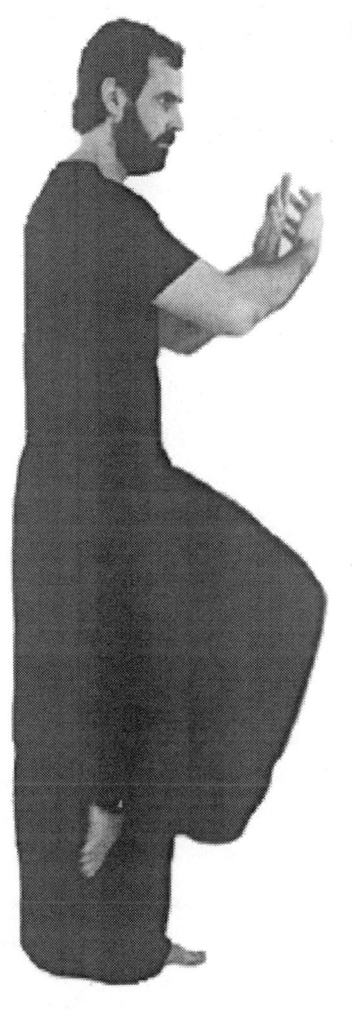

Cross and lift the arms while lifting the right foot. Your right hand is on the outside.

20

When we forsake trying to know, we have no more troubles. There is only a small difference between yes and no, good and ill. Perhaps we can move beyond the status quo and into a more expansive viewpoint.

128 FLAT SINGLE WHIP

Stay on the left foot as you begin to turn to the right. Stay pigeon-toed.

Wu Xing means the five states of change, sometimes called the five elements.

288 RUB RIGHT FOOT

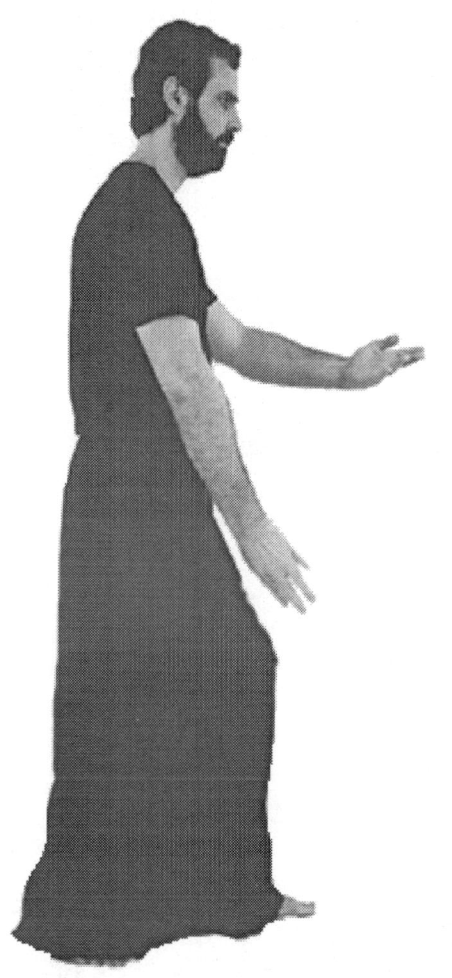

Shift forward.

Simplicity, non-interference and a trust in the Dao will do more to balance the world than the most well-intentioned meddling.

129 FLAT SINGLE WHIP

Turn as far as is comfortable.

The Wu Xing are earth, metal, water, wood and fire.

287 RUB RIGHT FOOT

Keep circling the right arm. Turn out the left toes.

19

Kindness, wisdom and morality cannot be forced on people. Only nature can guide people to virtue. The more we interfere, the more harm we do.

130 FLAT SINGLE WHIP

Begin to shift the weight to the right.

Earth is the center, the color yellow, late summer and the qualities of solidity and passivity.

286 RUB RIGHT FOOT

Shift back. Circle the right arm up and out while raising the left arm into a ward off position.

When the Dao is forgotten, loyalties turn to the family and the state. People act according to tradition, not to what is best.

131 FLAT SINGLE WHIP

Finish shifting the weight and swing the elbow out.

Metal is the west, the color white, the Autumn and the qualities of hardness and malleability.

285 STACK UP

Stack both hands up over the knee.

18
When the Dao is forgotten morality and kindness appear. Then come wisdom and cleverness. If someone is good, another is bad; if someone smart, another is stupid.

132 FLAT SINGLE WHIP

Strike with elbow is hidden in single whip.

Water is the north, the color black, the winter and the qualities of softness and fluidity.

284 STACK UP

Shift forward.

The perfect ruler successfully completes his work and the people believe that it was their own doing. You must have faith in the people for them to have faith in you.

133 FIST UNDER ELBOW

Pick the right foot up with the toes turned out as if walking around a corner.

Wood is the east, the color green, the spring and the qualities of springiness and growth.

283 STACK UP

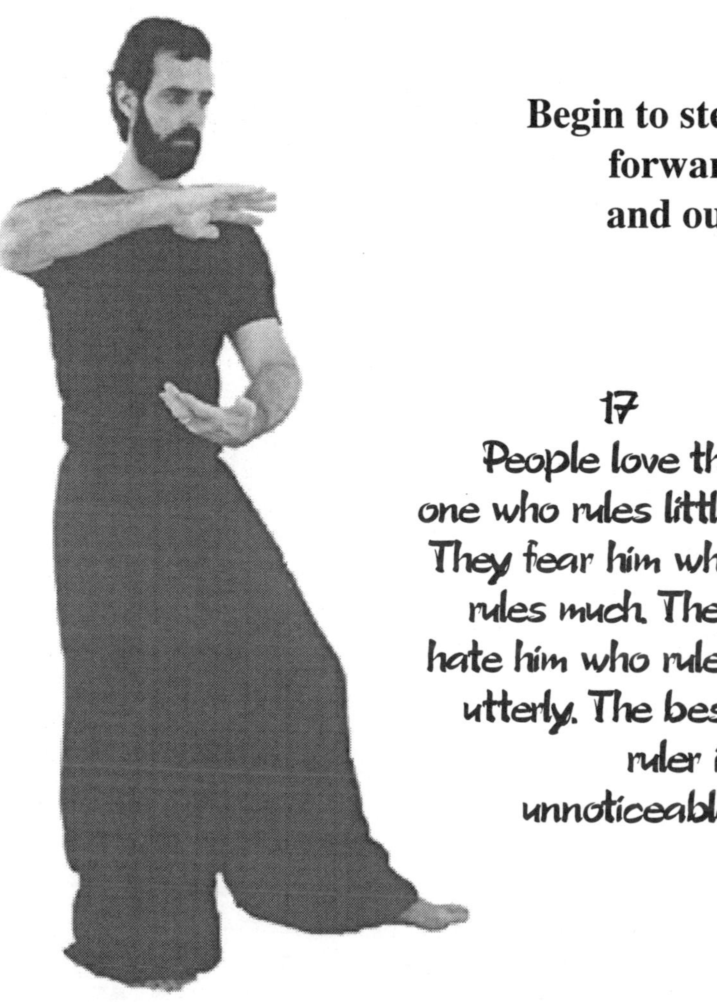

Begin to step forward and out.

17

People love the one who rules little. They fear him who rules much. They hate him who rules utterly. The best ruler is unnoticeable.

134 FIST UNDER ELBOW

**Move the
hand and
foot as one
unit but
let the
waist lead.**

*Fire is the south,
the color red,
the summer and
the qualities
of heat
and
consumption.*

282 HIGH PAT ON HORSE

Begin to turn the arms to the right.

To know that all things return to their source gives one great tolerance and empathy toward all things. This leads to the Dao, and the Dao is eternal.

135 FIST UNDER ELBOW

Set the foot down with the toes turned out.

The Wu Xing relate to each other in two cycles creation and control.

281 HIGH PAT ON HORSE

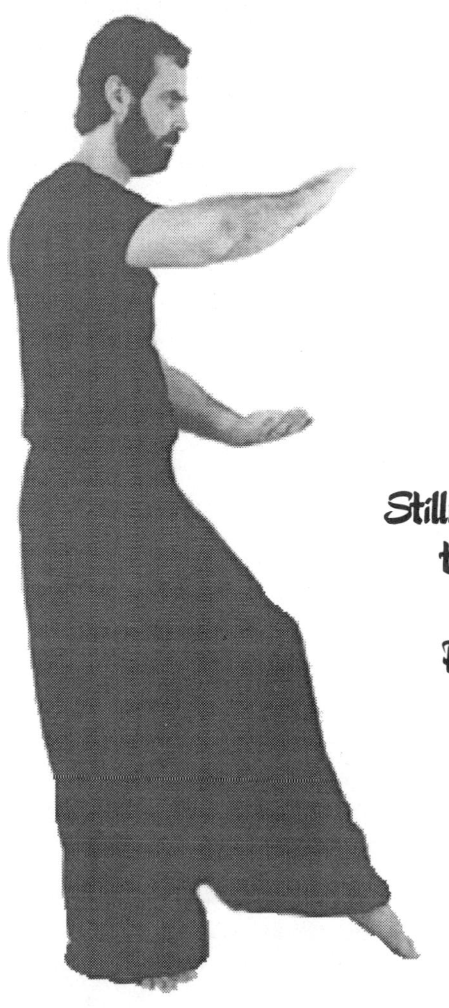

The left hand is under the horse's mouth while the right hand pats its forehead.

16

Stillness and void are the beginning and end of all things. Plants grow in the spring and are still in the winter. Stillness is a sign of completion.

136 FIST UNDER ELBOW

Begin the same movement with the right side.

Earth creates metal in the sense that metal is found in the earth.

280 HIGH PAT ON HORSE

Draw the left foot back; just the toes will touch the earth.

Those who follow the way of the ancient masters do not do so to exalt themselves. It is by being unexalted that they can afford to seem low and incomplete.

137 FIST UNDER ELBOW

Step forward.

Metal creates water in that metal becomes a liquid when heated, or in the way that water will condense on a metal surface.

279 HIGH PAT ON HORSE

138 FIST UNDER ELBOW

Swing the foot and arm in a gentle arc.

Water creates wood in the way the water will nourish the growth of a tree.

278 HIGH PAT ON HORSE

139 FIST UNDER ELBOW

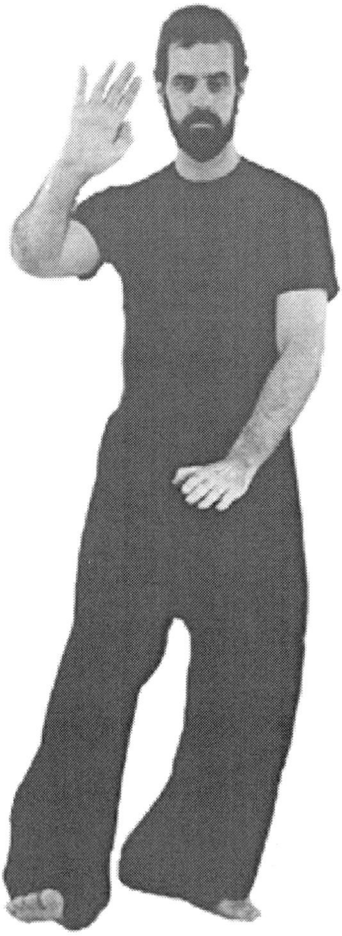

Set the foot down with the toes pointing straight forward.

Wood creates fire in that wood easily burns.

277 HIGH PAT ON HORSE

Shift back.

To make muddy
water clear,
let it stand
for a time.
It will
clear
of itself.

140 FIST UNDER ELBOW

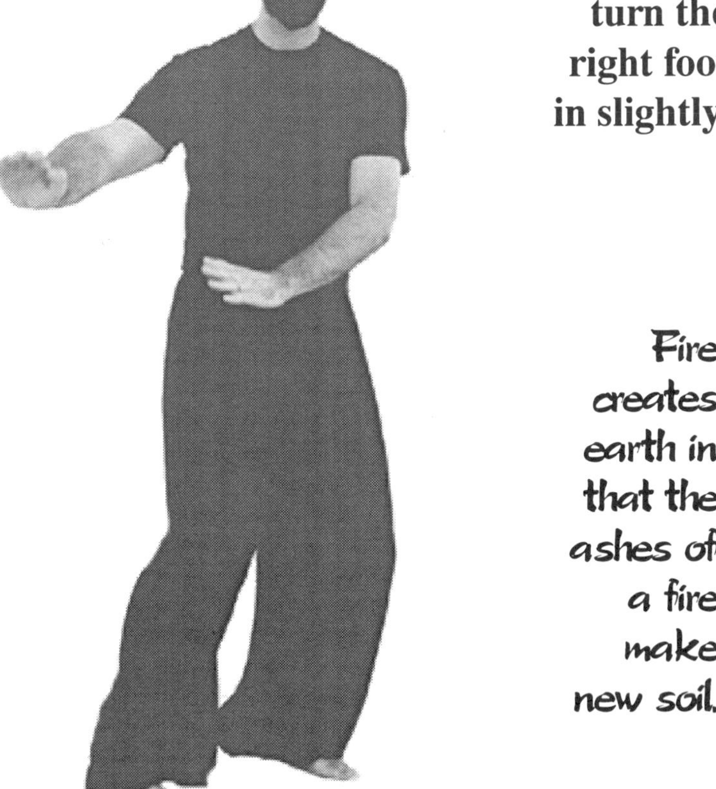

At the last moment turn the right foot in slightly.

Fire creates earth in that the ashes of a fire make new soil.

276 HIGH PAT ON HORSE

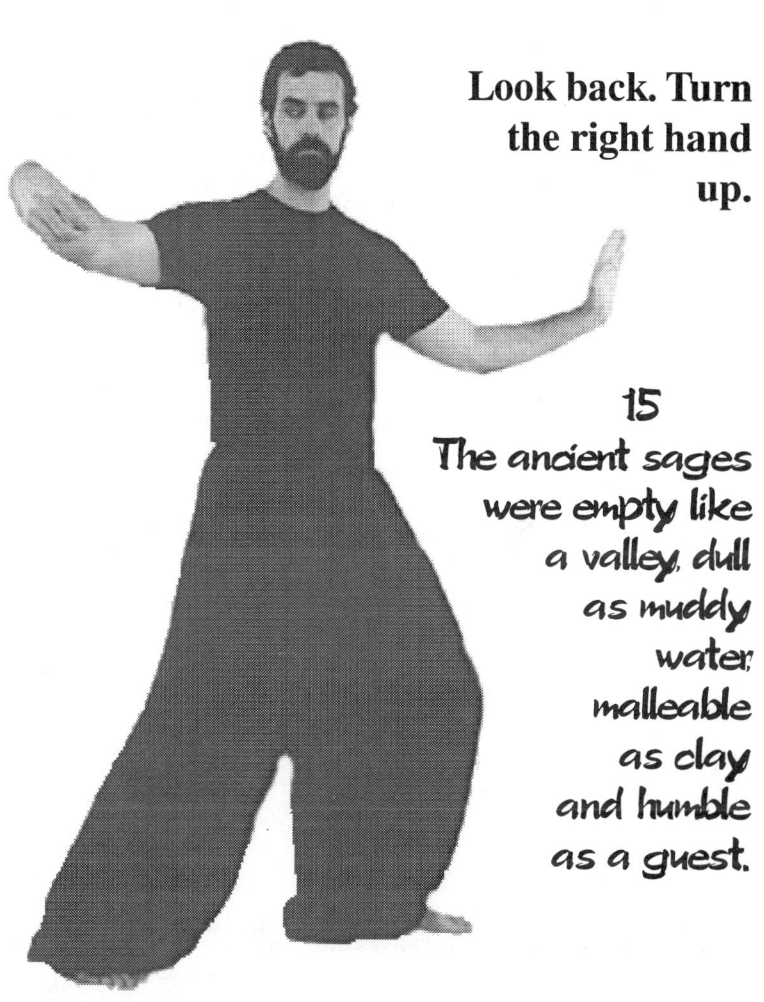

Look back. Turn the right hand up.

15

The ancient sages were empty like a valley, dull as muddy water, malleable as clay and humble as a guest.

141 FIST UNDER ELBOW

Form a fist with the right hand. The left arm and leg repeat the same swinging gesture.

Earth controls water by damming it and channeling it.

275 SINGLE WHIP

Push forward with the palm.

The Dao is the form of the formless. Although you cannot see the forest for the trees you can still build your house in it.

142 FIST UNDER ELBOW

Set just the heel down, keep all your weight back.

Water controls fire by extinguishing its flames and cooling its heat.

274 SINGLE WHIP

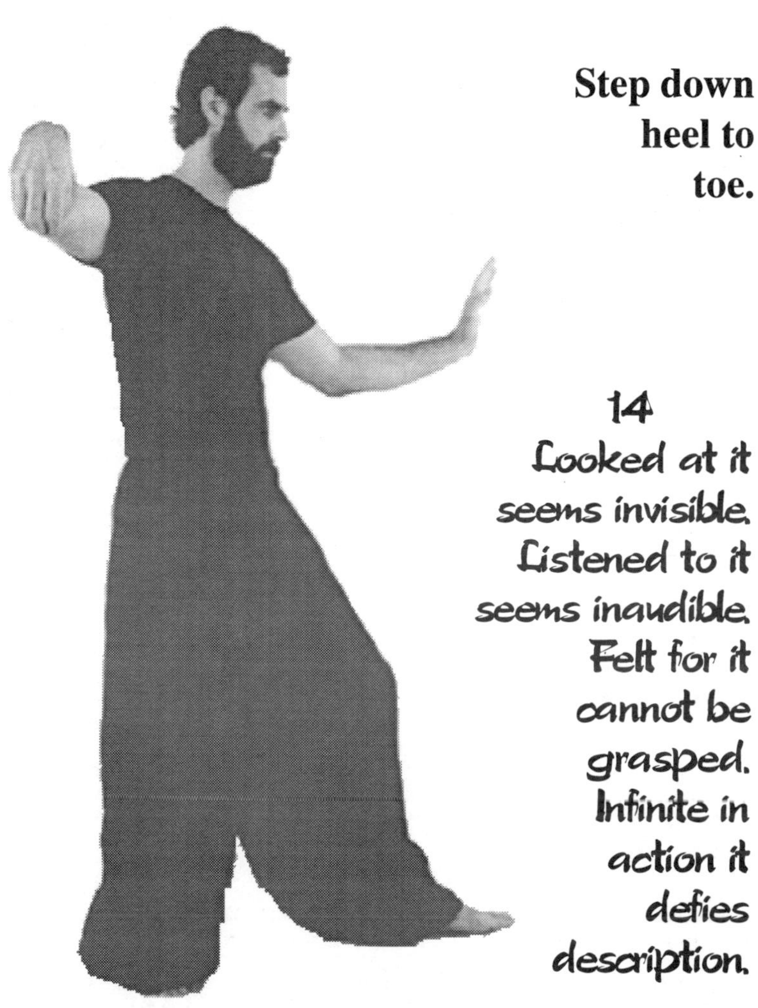

Step down heel to toe.

14

Looked at it seems invisible. Listened to it seems inaudible. Felt for it cannot be grasped. Infinite in action it defies description.

143 FIST UNDER ELBOW

The top of your fist will lightly touch your elbow.

Fire controls metal by melting it.

273 SINGLE WHIP

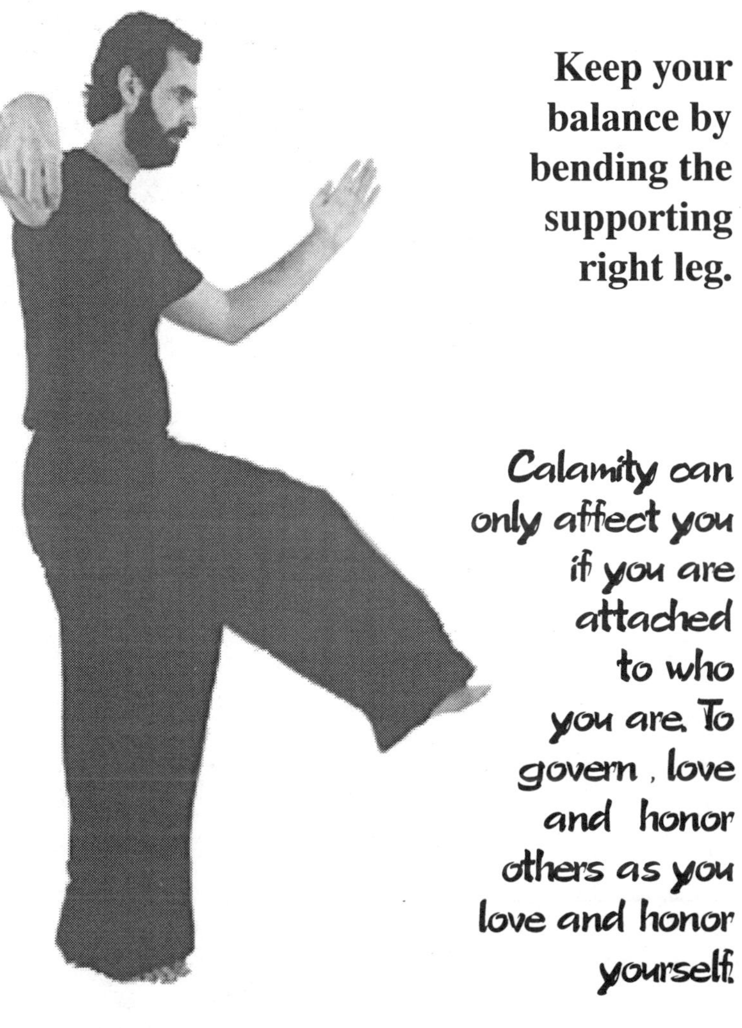

Keep your balance by bending the supporting right leg.

Calamity can only affect you if you are attached to who you are. To govern, love and honor others as you love and honor yourself.

144 REPULSE MONKEY

Begin to pick up the left foot.

Metal controls wood by cutting through it.

272 SINGLE WHIP

Lift the hand and foot in a sweeping gesture to the outside.

13

Success and failure are equally to be feared. Gaining success leads to fear of failure. Failure leads to regret.

145 REPULSE MONKEY

Relax the left arm.

Wood controls earth in the way that a tree's roots will break up the soil.

271 SINGLE WHIP

Shift to the right and extend the right hand.

The sage seeks to satisfy his spirit and true nature, not the craving of the senses.

146 REPULSE MONKEY

Lift the leg as high as is comfortable.

Each element has a Yin and a Yang aspect.

270 SINGLE WHIP

Keep the weight on the left as you twist to your right as far as is comfortable.

12
Color blinds the eye. Music deafens the ear. Flavors deaden the tongue. Desires dissolve the will.

147 REPULSE MONKEY

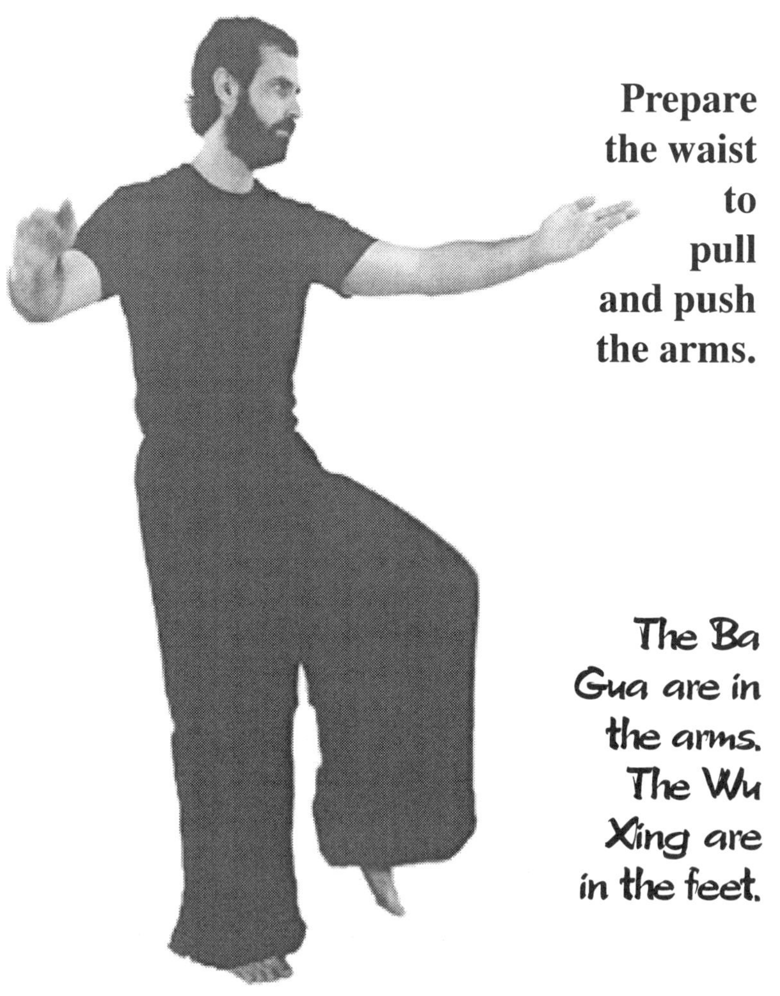

Prepare the waist to pull and push the arms.

The Ba Gua are in the arms. The Wu Xing are in the feet.

269 SINGLE WHIP

Turn to the left. The right foot is pigeon-toed.

We fashion objects and things for their potential, but it is the lack of a thing that we actually want.

148 REPULSE MONKEY

Reach back with the toes.

The Wu Xing are expressed in the form through movement in five directions.

268 SINGLE WHIP

Gather the fingers together.

11

The usefulness of a cup is in its emptiness. The usefulness of a window is in its lack of substance. The most important part of a wheel is the hole for the axle.

149 REPULSE MONKEY

Set the foot down toe to heel; pull with the left, push with the right.

To move forward is metal, retreat is wood, left is water, right is fire and central equilibrium is earth.

267 CLOUD HANDS

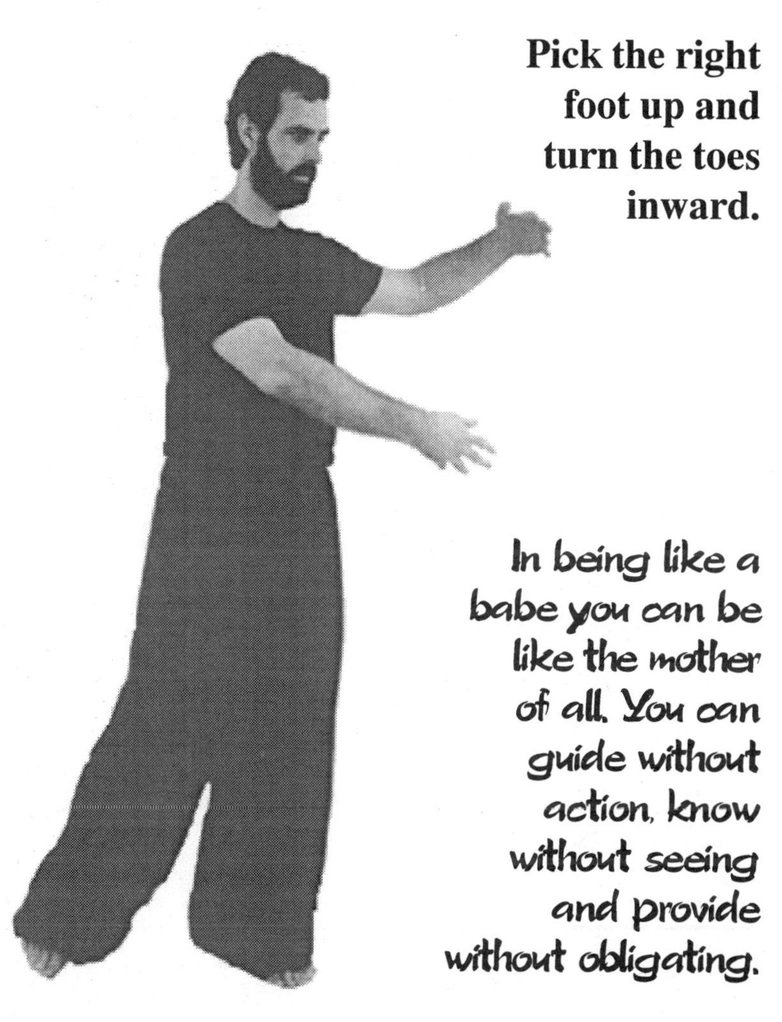

Pick the right foot up and turn the toes inward.

In being like a babe you can be like the mother of all. You can guide without action, know without seeing and provide without obligating.

150 REPULSE MONKEY

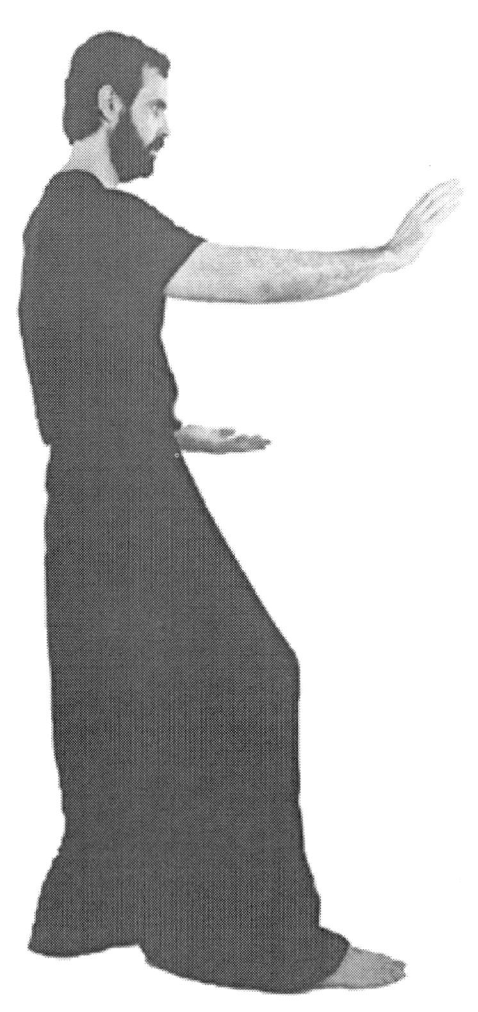

The movement's full name is fall back to drive away the monkey.

If the opponent's movement is fiery, neutralize it by being watery.

266 CLOUD HANDS

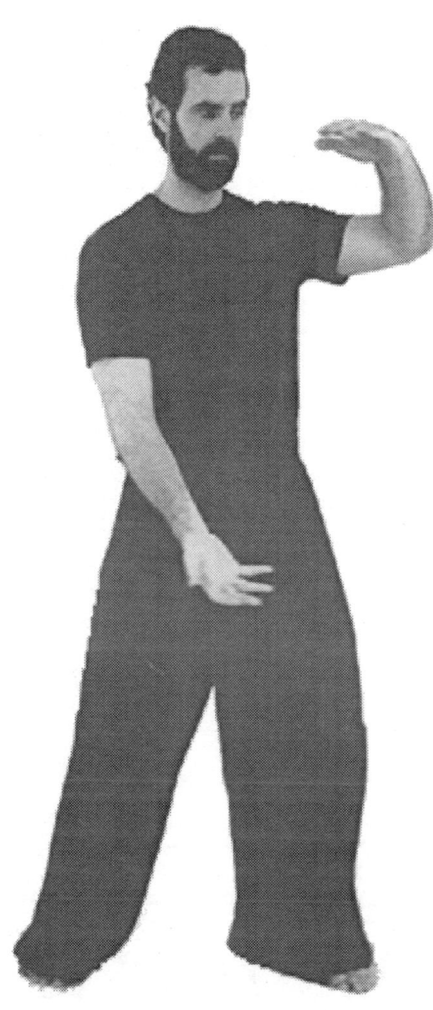

Shift the weight but do not bring in the right foot this time.

10

When the mind and body are one, when the attention is wholly on the Qi, when the mind is clear of illusions we can be as supple and perfect as a babe.

151 REPULSE MONKEY

Relax the right arm and begin to turn the palm up.

Metallic behavior may create water in the opponent.

265 CLOUD HANDS

Step out.

When the work is finished and the sage is becoming known, he withdraws. This is the way of heaven.

152 REPULSE MONKEY

The left arm cycles up and out towards the ear.

Study of the Wu Xing teaches both footwork and strategy.

264 CLOUD HANDS

Use the waist to move the arms. Shift the weight to the right foot.

9

It is better not to fill a cup to the top than to try to carry it when full. If you keep testing the strength of a branch it will break. When gold fills your house you cannot keep it safe.

153 REPULSE MONKEY

Roll onto the foot and sink the weight down.

The five directions combined with the eight gates form the thirteen postures of Tai Chi.

263 CLOUD HANDS

Keep the knees bent and the elbows relaxed.

The worth of a house is in its vacancy, that of the mind is in its stillness, that of a movement in its timing. And when a worthy one is content with the low places no one finds defect in him.

154 REPULSE MONKEY

Shift back as you pull and push.

Dao means way. It refers to process: the way things happen, the essential how of the universe.

262 CLOUD HANDS

Begin to bring the right foot in.

8

The ultimate virtue is like water. It benefits all life and keeps to the low places. The way of water is like the way of the Dao.

155 REPULSE MONKEY

The movement is the same as before.

Daoism is an ancient Chinese philosophy that seeks to explain the way.

261 CLOUD HANDS

Shift the weight with the hands; timing is very important.

The sage places himself last and finds himself first. Because he has no personal desires his desires are realized.

156 REPULSE MONKEY

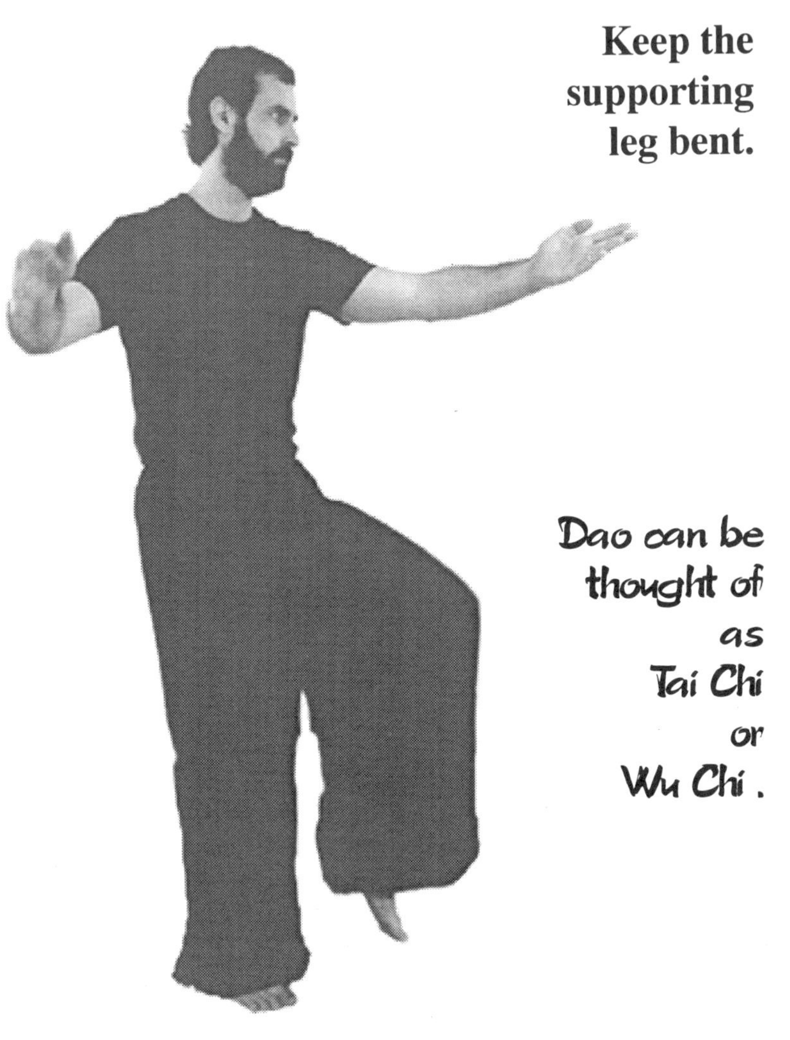

Keep the supporting leg bent.

Dao can be thought of as Tai Chi or Wu Chi .

260 CLOUD HANDS

Step out to the side as you did before.

7

Heaven and earth endure because they do not exist of and for themselves.

157 REPULSE MONKEY

Keep the elbows relaxed.

Dao is Wu Chi in that it is the source of everything. It is Tai Chi in that it describes all process.

259 CLOUD HANDS

Shift to your right. Wave hands like clouds drifting by.

Constant and infinite is the Dao. Yet its touch is so light you do not even realize it is there.

158 REPULSE MONKEY

Exhale as you shift the weight back.

Tai Chi and all its relevant philosophy is Daoist in origin. One cannot study Tai Chi without studying Daoism.

258 CLOUD HANDS

The feet are right next to each other. The cloud hand sequence repeats itself three times.

6

The emptiness of the Dao is the emptiness of the womb. It is the potential of all things.

159 REPULSE MONKEY

Move smoothly and without pause.

To live in harmony with the Dao is the ultimate aim of practicing the art of Tai Chi.

257 CLOUD HANDS

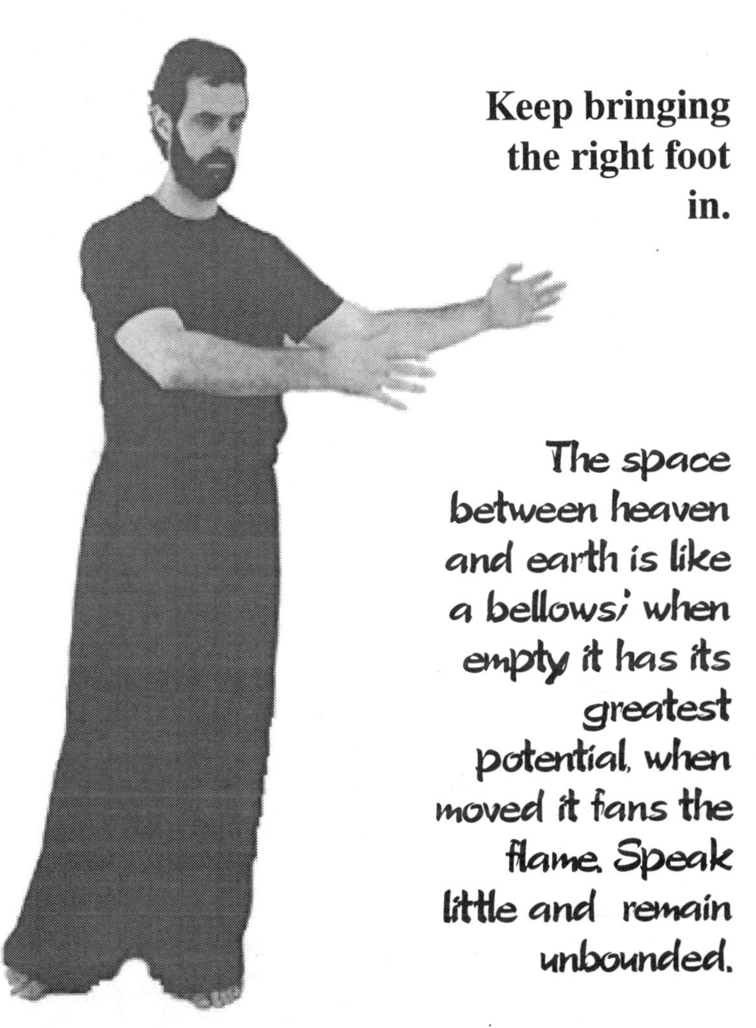

Keep bringing the right foot in.

The space between heaven and earth is like a bellows; when empty it has its greatest potential, when moved it fans the flame. Speak little and remain unbounded.

160 DIAGONAL FLYING

One arm circles up, one circles down. Pick up the right foot.

Daoist philosophy maintains that to live out of harmony with the Dao would make life very difficult, like swimming upstream.

256 CLOUD HANDS

The hands move as if holding a ball, turning it over while moving it from one side of the body to the other.

5

Heaven and
earth do not act
out of kindness.
They are ruthlessly
indifferent to the
desires of people.
The sage treats
people with the
same indifference.

161 DIAGONAL FLYING

Keep the arms circling. Step behind your left foot.

Through the symbolism of the Tai Chi form we can understand the Dao.

255 CLOUD HANDS

Walk through cloud hands like a crab. Keep the knees bent as you shuffle left for the entire sequence.

We should round our edges, untie our knots, dim our lights and shape ourselves to the will of others. The Dao is still and pure; even God is its child.

162 DIAGONAL FLYING

Begin to turn to the right diagonal. Shift the weight to the right foot.

Through an understanding of the movements of the Tai Chi form we can learn to change our behavior to better align ourselves with the Dao.

254 CLOUD HANDS

Begin to step the right foot in towards the left.

4

The Dao is like an empty cup and when we use it we must be wary of its fullness. It is infinite and incomprehensible. It is the mother of all.

163 DIAGONAL FLYING

Pick up the left foot and turn the toes inward.

The most famous Daoist scholar was Lao Tzu. Lao Tzu means old master or old philosopher

253 CLOUD HANDS

Shift the weight as the hands pass by.

The sage leads people by filling their bellies, relaxing their minds, encouraging their flexibility and nurturing their security. He brings them to rest in the Dao where nothing need be done.

164 DIAGONAL FLYING

Begin to shift the weight left. Keep the arms away from the body.

Lao Tzu wrote a book entitled The Dao De Jing, which means The Book of the Way and its Virtues.

252 CLOUD HANDS

Begin to step the left foot out to the side.

3

If you prize that which is in abundance no one need steal. If they know the joy of the ordinary they will be content.

165 DIAGONAL FLYING

Begin to pick up your right foot. Lead with the shoulder.

The Dao De Jing teaches a method of governing oneself and others according to Daoist principles.

251 CLOUD HANDS

Shift the weight to the right foot as the hands drift to the right.

The sage does without doing, instructs without speaking. All things arise from the Dao and are nurtured by it. Yet it lays no claim on them. The work is done without expectation and without conceit.

166 DIAGONAL FLYING

Step to the diagonal.

The philosophy in the Dao De Jing applies perfectly to the practice of Tai Chi.

250 CLOUD HANDS

Circle the hands as if you were turning over a large ball. The feet are close together but the weight is still on the left foot.

2

To know beauty is to
know ugliness,
to know
competence is
to know incompetence.
Being and nonbeing
give birth to one another,
high and low describe
one another, long and
short contrast one another,
before and after follow
one another.

167 DIAGONAL FLYING

Turn the body to the right as you shift forward.

Another important Daoist writer was Chuang Tzu. His writings are fundamental to Daoist thought.

249 CLOUD HANDS

Begin to bring the right foot in to the left foot.

Only without desire can we penetrate the mystery. Where the mystery is the deepest is the door to all that is elusive and wonderful.

168 DIAGONAL FLYING

Follow through and begin to pick up the left foot.

Chuang Tzu once dreamed he was a butterfly and upon waking wondered if he was then a butterfly dreaming he was a man.

248 CLOUD HANDS

Shift back to the left.

Having no name it gave birth to heaven and earth. Having a name it is the mother of all. Arising from the same source in function we see their differences.

169 DIAGONAL FLYING

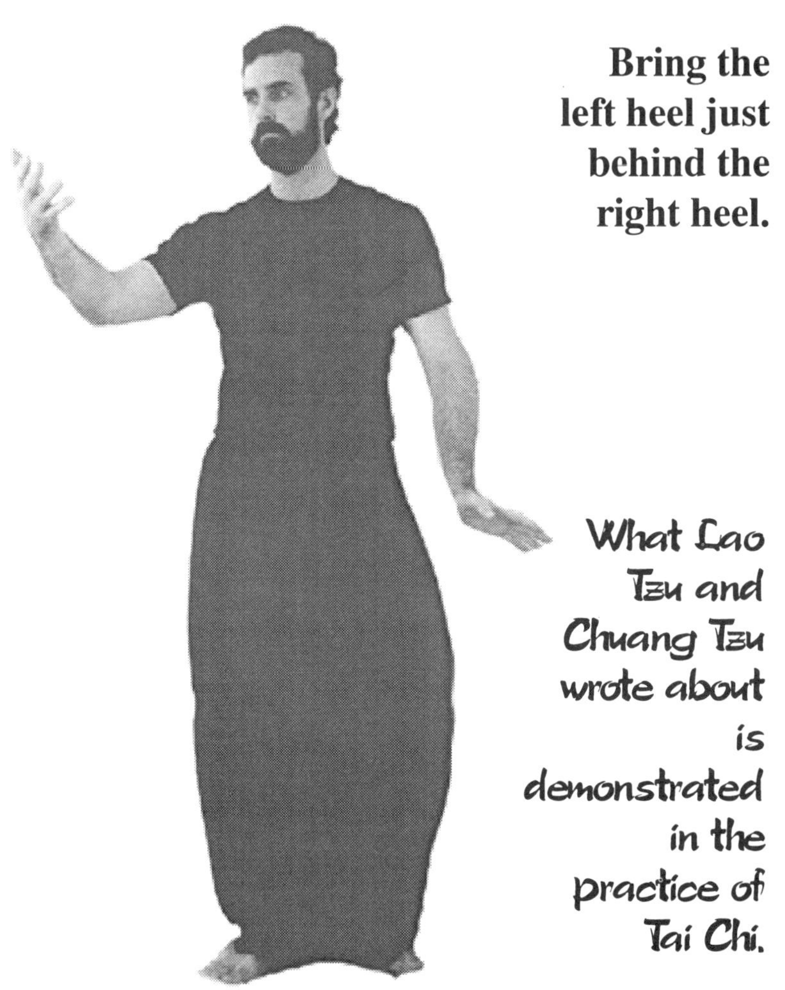

Bring the left heel just behind the right heel.

What Lao Tzu and Chuang Tzu wrote about is demonstrated in the practice of Tai Chi.

247 CLOUD HANDS

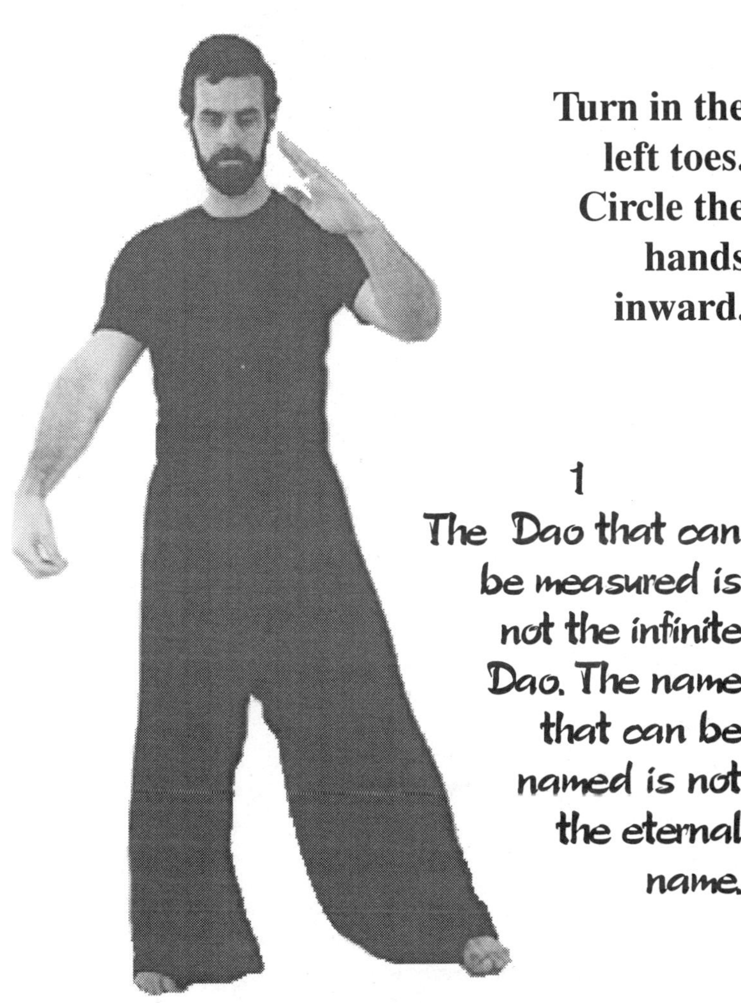

Turn in the left toes. Circle the hands inward.

1

The Dao that can be measured is not the infinite Dao. The name that can be named is not the eternal name.

170 PLAY THE HARP

Shift back and circle the hands out, then in.

To understand with the mind is one thing. To have experience is another. To have both knowledge and experience is wisdom.

246 CLOUD HANDS

Shift back to the right.

The Dao De Jing of Lao Tzu.

171 PLAY THE HARP

Begin to pick up the right foot and bring it in front you.

The practice of Tai Chi integrates the disciplines of the mind and the disciplines of the body, creating the most complete wisdom.

245 SINGLE WHIP

Follow through.

There may well be hundreds of styles and variations of Tai Chi. Yet all styles originate from the thirteen postures and are in essence the same.

172 PLAY THE HARP

Just the heel of the right foot touches the earth.

Daoism and Tai Chi often rely on the use of symbols to teach concepts that are very difficult to express in words.

244 SINGLE WHIP

Round the arms and the chest.

A student of both Yang and the Chens created another Wu style. It is known for its simplicity and minimalist approach.

173 PLAY THE HARP

Keep the weight back as you strum the harp.

This is called the Tai Chi emblem.

243 SINGLE WHIP

Exhale as you begin to shift forward.

The second most popular style is the Wu style. Similar in look and feel to Yang, it was developed by Yang's student.

174 PLAY THE HARP

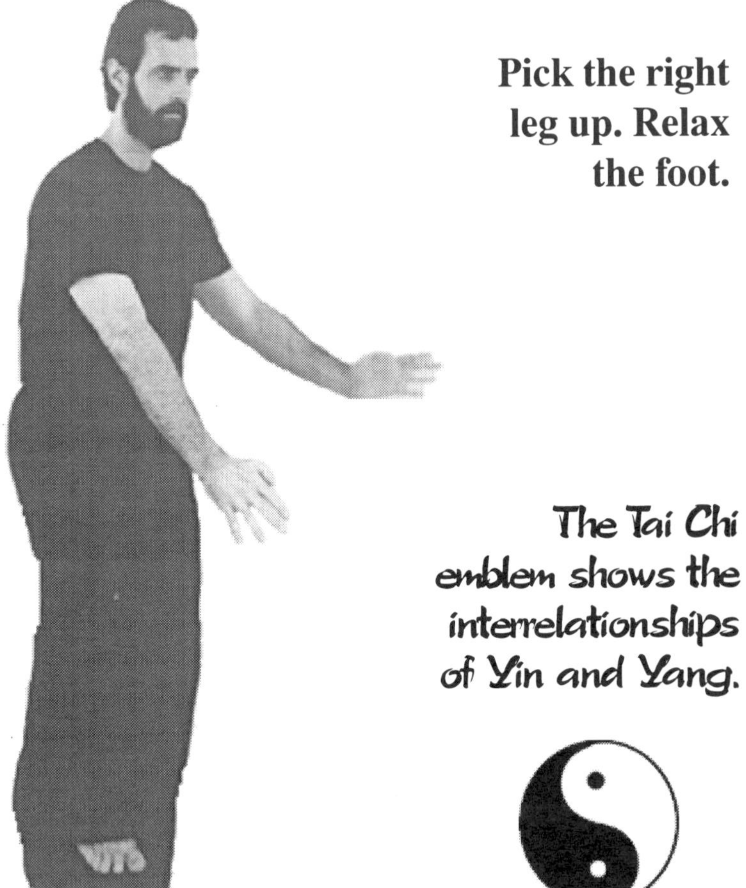

Pick the right leg up. Relax the foot.

The Tai Chi emblem shows the interrelationships of Yin and Yang.

242 SINGLE WHIP

Inhale and balance on the right leg.

175 SHOULDER STRIKE

Balance, feel your weight sink straight through the left foot.

The black represents Yin. The white represents Yang.

241 SINGLE WHIP

The hand and foot move together.

After learning hand forms students may learn weapon forms, such as sword, saber and staff.

176 SHOULDER STRIKE

Lead with the shoulder.

The Yin and Yang portions are shaped so as to indicate that they are in motion.

240 SINGLE WHIP

Push out the right hand. The right foot is still turned in.

Practice of the forms, push hands and da lu eventually leads the student into free sparring practice.

177 WHITE CRANE

Begin to lift the left foot.

Where the black Yin portion is at the fullest a small dot of Yang appears. It grows until at its fullest a small dot of Yin appears.

239 SINGLE WHIP

Begin to shift the weight to the right foot.

Da Lu is a training exercise in which two players attack and defend themselves using the techniques of the four corners: pull, split, elbow and shoulder.

178 WHITE CRANE

Separate the hands high and low. Begin to step forward.

The emblem shows that the extreme of Yin is the creation of Yang and vice versa.

238 SINGLE WHIP

Turn the waist to the right. Keep your weight left.

Push hands is a common training exercise. In pushing hands two players compete in trying to uproot each other using the techniques of ward off, roll back, press and push.

179 WHITE CRANE

Deflect away from the face and belly.

There is no process the Tai Chi emblem does not describe.

237 RAINBOW

The weight is on the left foot. Gather the fingers of the right hand together.

The Yang style also contains a two-person form in which two players move through a prearranged mock fight, utilizing movements from both the slow and fast form.

180 WHITE CRANE

Only the toe of the left foot touches the earth.

The Tai Chi emblem illustrates what the Tai Chi form demonstrates.

236 RAINBOW

Keep turning the toes in.

It is little known that Yang style contains a fast form. The fast form teaches applications of the slow form movements that require quick, light and nimble actions.

181 WHITE CRANE

Chop the right hand straight down the middle of your body.

This shows the relationship of Tai Chi to the Ba Gua.

235 RAINBOW

Bring the toes with the hands.

Moving slowly does not inhibit the ability to move quickly. However if you only move quickly many things, such as a firm root, a relaxed body and a meditative mind, will take much more time to develop. Slower can be faster.

182 BRUSH KNEE

Circle the hands to protect the body.

This is another arrangement of Tai Chi and Ba Gua.

234 RAINBOW

Flow smoothly from the push to the rainbow.

Yang found that practicing the form slowly created great softness and sensitivity. It also allowed the students to relax, concentrate and develop their Qi.

183 BRUSH KNEE

Keep circling the hands.

This diagram shows the interrelationships of the Wu Xing.

233 DOUBLE PUSH

Like the tide moving up the beach.

Yang style Tai Chi is known for its comfortable, slow, simple movements and is overwhelmingly the most popular style. It is the style presented in this book.

184 BRUSH KNEE

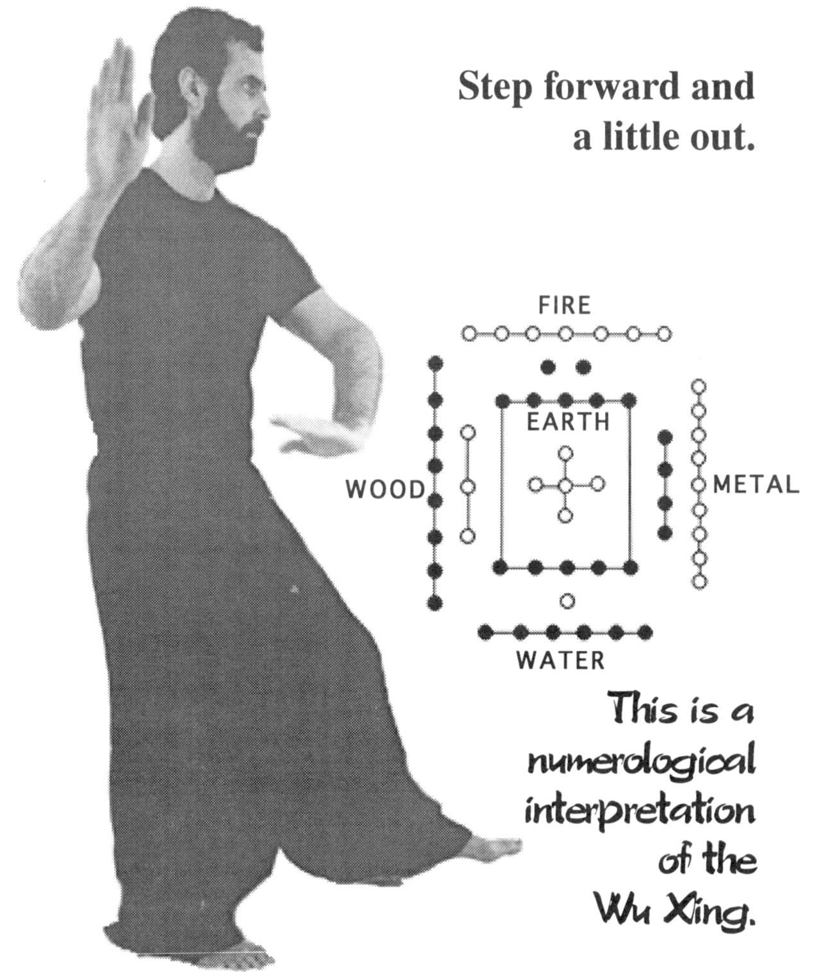

Step forward and a little out.

This is a numerological interpretation of the Wu Xing.

232 DOUBLE PUSH

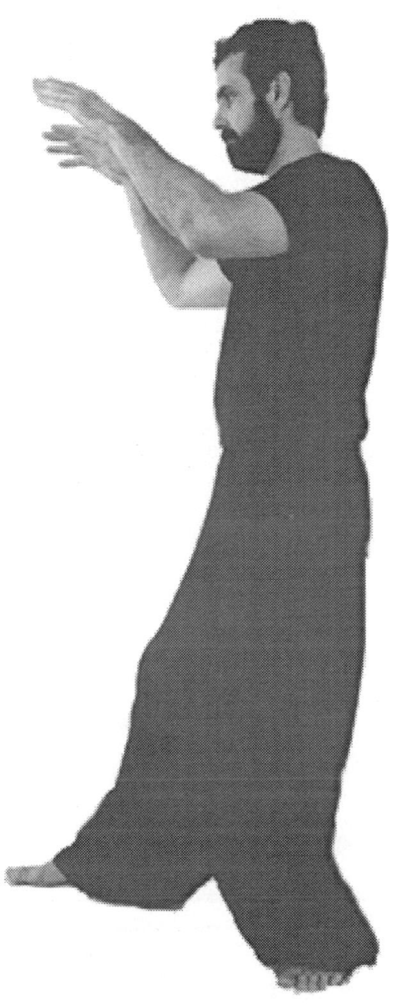

Like a wave rising up from the sea.

Yang found that his new, softer, slower version of the form was surprisingly effective. His sons and grandsons continued to develop this approach, resulting in the form we have today.

185 BRUSH KNEE

Shift forward,
pull and push.

This is the Wu Xing numbers in relation to the Ba Gua.

231 DOUBLE PUSH

Relax the wrists. Sink the elbows.

Because the royal family were Manchus, the despised oppressors of the Chinese, Yang modified his Tai Chi, de-emphasizing the martial aspects.

186 BRUSH KNEE

Relax; become soft.

Animals are also used as symbols and models to help us to understand and experience the concepts and movements of Tai Chi.

230 PRESS

Follow through. Press the left hand lightly to the right forearm.

Yang's reputation drew the attention of the emperor, who conscripted Yang to teach at the royal court. This gave Yang's style great prestige and renown.

187 DROP NEEDLE

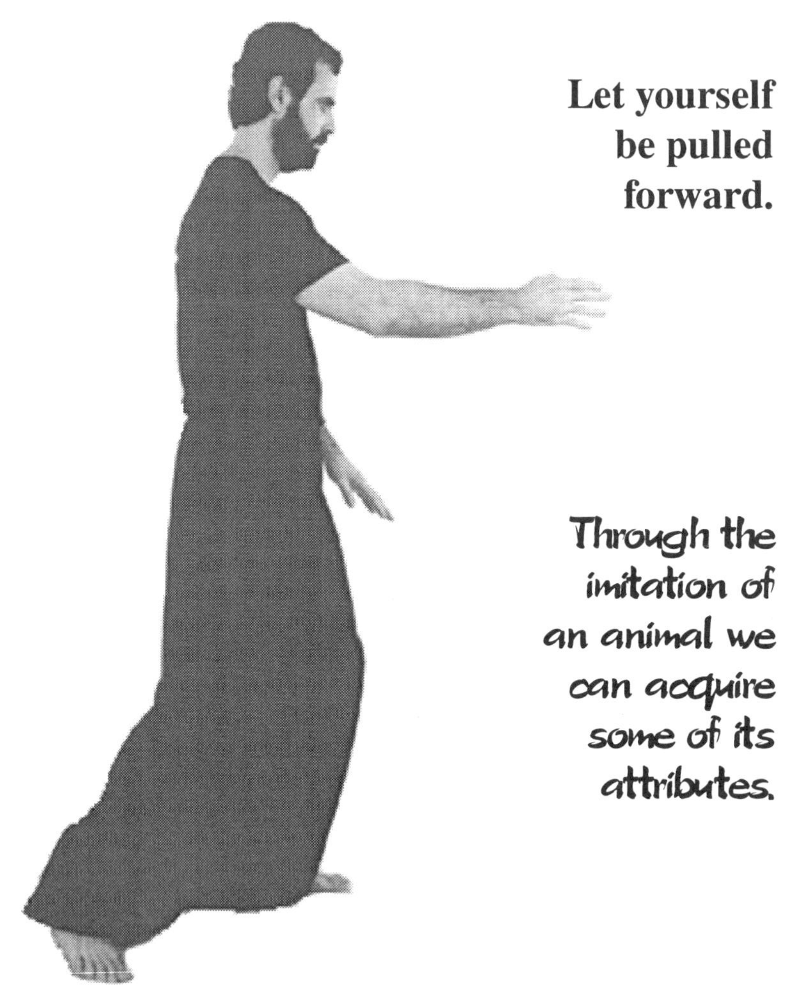

Let yourself be pulled forward.

Through the imitation of an animal we can acquire some of its attributes.

229 PRESS

Turn the waist to the right when you press.

After mastering the Chen style, Yang travelled throughout China matching his skills against the best fighters of the day. Because he never lost and everyone respected him he was called No-Rival Yang.

188 DROP NEEDLE

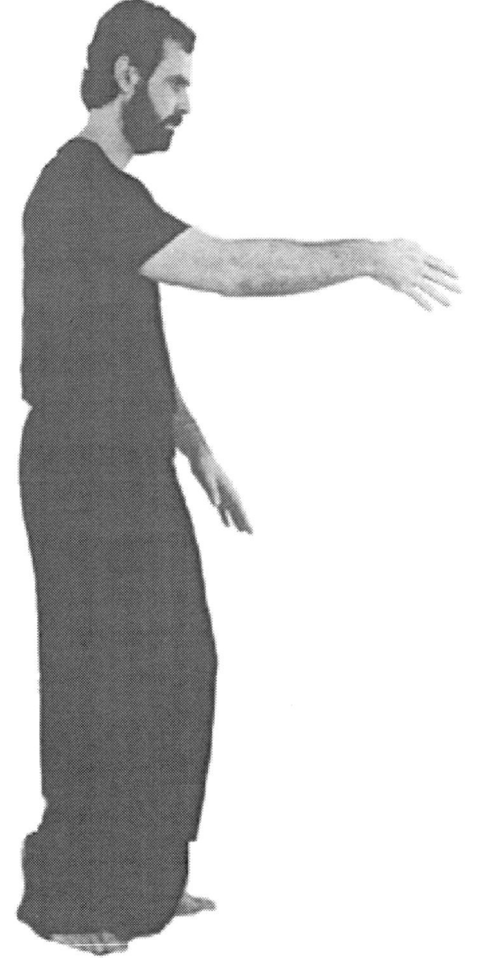

Bring the right heel to the left heel.

The attributes of an animal can exemplify a Daoist principle.

228 ROLL BACK

Roll back with the waist first; let the arms follow.

After secretly observing the Chens in practice, Yang was able to defeat many of the best Chen fighters. Yang was thereafter taught openly and fully.

189 DROP NEEDLE

Step back again and start circling the hands.

A monkey has a flexible, curious and adaptive nature and so corresponds to water.

227 ROLL BACK

Yield to overcome. Weakness creates strength. Yin creates Yang.

A man named Yang Lu Shan wished to study with the Chen fighters but was refused. He remained with the Chens as a field hand in hopes of one day being accepted.

190 DROP NEEDLE

Begin to pick up the left foot

A bear has a solid, slow and ponderous nature and so corresponds to earth.

226 ROLL BACK

Exactly the same as the very first roll back.

There are two styles of Chen Tai Chi Chuan widely practiced today: the older original style and a newer modified version.

191 DROP NEEDLE

Keep the left foot light and sink straight down.

A tiger is strong, fierce and ruthless and so corresponds to metal.

225 WARD OFF

Shift forward and ward off right.

The Chen style includes both fast and slow movements and is very dynamic in appearance. Its fighting spirit is obvious and it requires great stamina and flexibility.

192 DROP NEEDLE

Sink only as far as comfort allows.

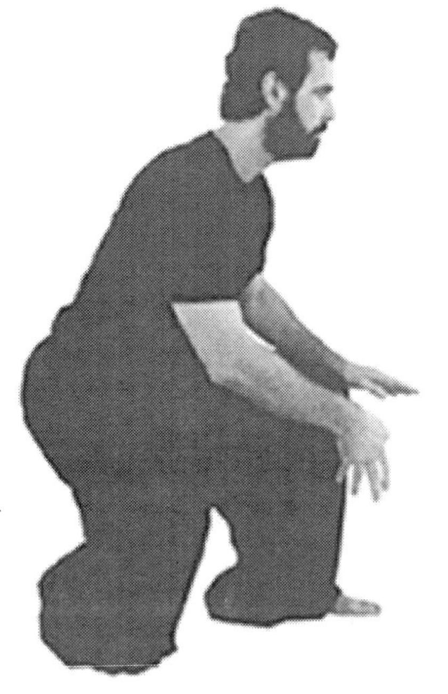

A snake has the ability to renew itself through shedding its skin and so corresponds to wood.

224 WARD OFF

The hands circle past one another.

Of the Tai Chi Chuan that existed before the origin of the Chen style very little knowledge remains.

193 DROP NEEDLE

Turn the palm up and towards your face.

The stag is quick and passionate and so corresponds to fire.

223 WARD OFF

The left hand presses down and back; the right hand moves up and forward.

Wang stayed with the Chens and modified their art to accord with Daoist principles. The resulting Chen style of Tai Chi Chuan is the ancestor of all the existing styles of Tai Chi Chuan.

194 DROP NEEDLE

Keep turning the palm in the same direction.

Many of the movements of Tai Chi are named after animals to provide insight into the spirit of the movement.

222 WARD OFF

Begin to step forward.

A Daoist named Wang was passing through the Chen village where he observed the Chens practicing their family martial art called cannon fist. Wang derided their art and easily defeated the best of the Chen fighters.

195 FAN ON THE BACK

Keep turning the palm as you begin to raise the arm.

Since Tai Chi is based on the movements of nature it is appropriate to imitate the movements of animals while doing the form.

221 WARD OFF

The hands are circling inward now.

Tai Chi Chuan as we know it today began with the Chen family during the Ching dynasty.

196 FAN ON THE BACK

Begin to rise and bring the left hand up.

When we drop low to the earth or make subtle fluid movements of the arm we are using snake movements.

220 WARD OFF

Shift forward and begin to step forward.

Although Tai Chi Chuan was probably developed over many years by many people from both Daoist and Shaolin martial arts, we can honor them through honoring Chang San Feng.

197 FAN ON THE BACK

Step slightly forward and out.

When we stand on one leg or make large circular movements of the arm we are moving in the spirit of the crane.

219 TWO BIRDS FLY OFF

Keep circling the arms.

There are several stories as to how Chang San Feng created Tai Chi Chuan: that he learned it in a dream, that he was taught by a Daoist hermit and that he was inspired by the sight of a snake and a crane in combat.

198 FAN ON THE BACK

Shift forward, pull and push.

The coiling and uncoiling of the waist is the use of dragon movement.

218 TWO BIRDS FLY OFF

One hand circles high, one low. Turn the left toes out with the movement of the left arm.

A wandering Daoist named Chang San Feng is credited with founding Tai Chi Chuan. Chang San Feng was born during the Sung dynasty and was reported to have lived more than two hundred years.

199 TURN AND CHOP

As you shift to your right foot, turn in the left toes.

Through the slowness of the movements, the practitioner acquires some of the energy of the turtle.

217 TWO BIRDS FLY OFF

Rest your fist on the palm of the left hand; shift back.

Buddhism was centered at the Shaolin temple; Daoism was centered around Wu Dang mountain. Both philosophies influenced each other.

200 TURN AND CHOP

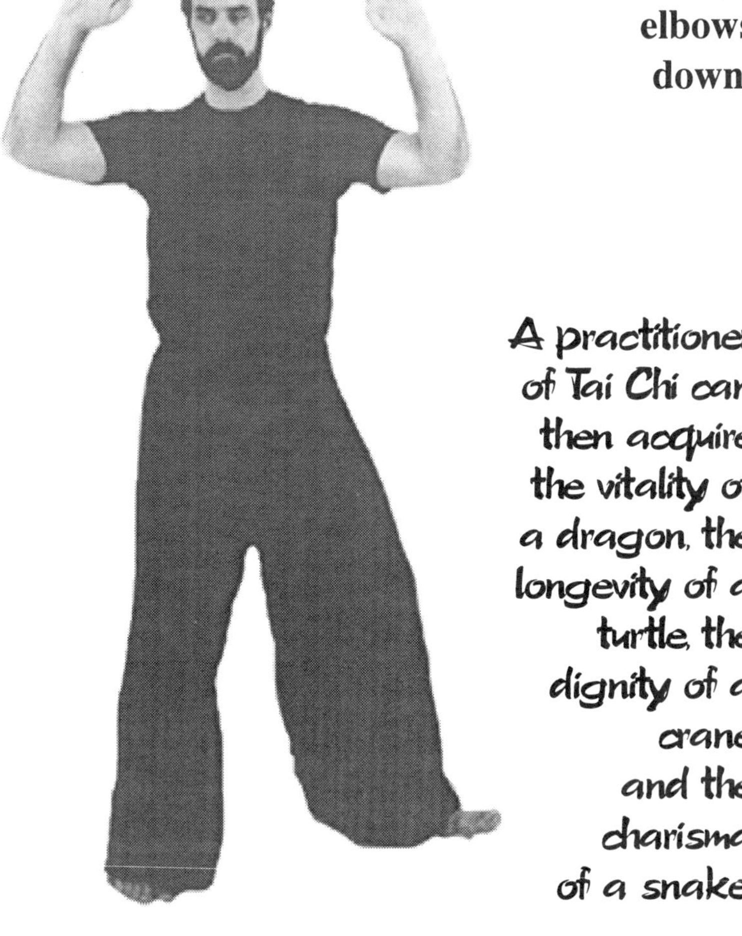

Hands up, elbows down.

A practitioner of Tai Chi can then acquire the vitality of a dragon, the longevity of a turtle, the dignity of a crane and the charisma of a snake.

216 PARRY AND PUNCH

Follow through but do not over extend.

Shaolin martial arts became very famous and spread throughout China, Influencing almost all Oriental martial arts.

201 TURN AND CHOP

Shift the weight and lean slightly.

The art of Tai Chi is the study of the universe and you as a reflection of it.

215 PARRY AND PUNCH

Shift forward and bring the left hand in to support the punch.

Da Mo found the Shaolin monks to be in poor physical health. To strengthen them for the rigors of meditation Da Mo, who had been of the warrior caste, taught the monks martial arts.

202 TURN AND CHOP

Begin to shift to the left foot.

We contain all the aspects of the divine and the mundane. The practice of the form can prove this to you.

214 PARRY AND PUNCH

Begin to punch.

Martial arts began in China when a Buddhist monk named Da Mo travelled from India to the Shaolin temple in China to teach Buddhism.

203 TURN AND CHOP

Close the right hand into a loose fist.

The miraculousness of the art of Tai Chi is in the miracle of everyday experience.

213 PARRY AND PUNCH

Keep extending the left arm as you begin to step forward.

The words Kung Fu and Wu Shu also refer to martial arts and so to Tai Chi Chuan as well.

204 TURN AND CHOP

Both hands are circling, the left hand outward, the right hand inward.

The practice of Tai Chi can teach us a way to let go of the fears and habits that filter out the miracle of everyday life.

212 PARRY AND PUNCH

Shift forward and extend the left arm.

All the movements of Tai Chi Chuan are designed for self-defense. However, it might take many years of practice to be able to successfully apply the movements.

205 TURN AND CHOP

Step a little to the outside.

Tai Chi teaches resources and strategies that can enable the practitioner to have new and better choices of behavior and attitude.

211 PARRY AND PUNCH

Set the foot down turned out.

The art of Tai Chi Chuan applies natural law as seen through Daoist metaphysics to personal combat.

206 TURN AND CHOP

Bring the fist down first; then the hand follows.

Tai Chi is an art of transmutation. Fear becomes confidence, anger becomes compassion, violence becomes harmony and weakness becomes strength.

210 PARRY AND PUNCH

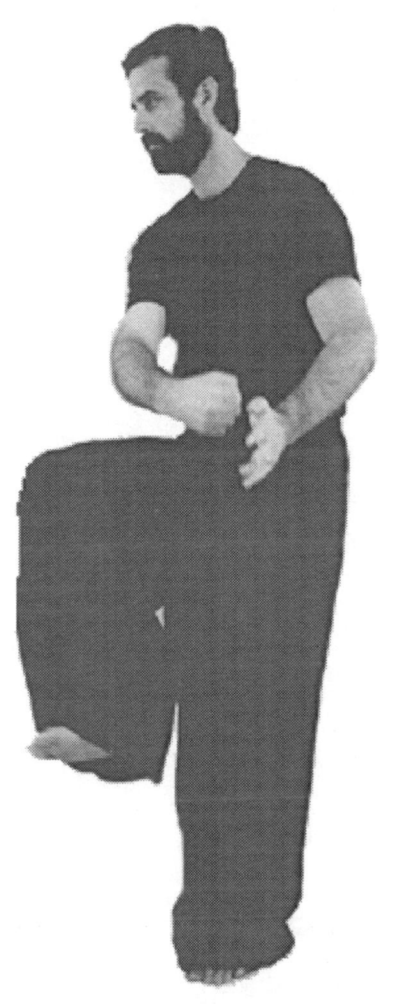

Continue the roll back movement, circling the hand up and in front of you.

Tai Chi Chuan means a martial art based on the principles of the supreme ultimate process of the universe.

207 TURN AND CHOP

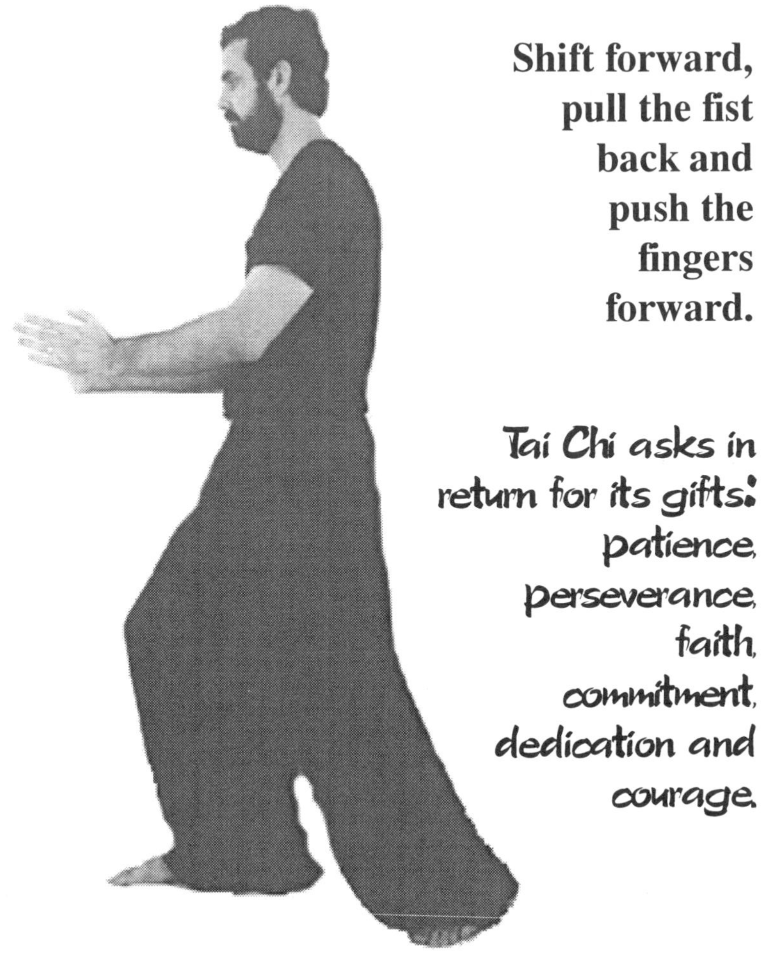

Shift forward, pull the fist back and push the fingers forward.

Tai Chi asks in return for its gifts: patience, perseverance, faith, commitment, dedication and courage.

209 ROLL BACK

Yield, redirect and strike all in one movement.

Tai Chi Chuan means supreme ultimate fist. Chuan or fist designates a martial art.

208 ROLL BACK

Keep the fist as you roll back.